VINCENZO DONATIELLO

Smile

A Modern Dictionary for Waiters

Preface by Enzo and Paolo Vizzari

ISBN: 9798584711207

TABLE OF CONTENTS

SDcw6FwPhX

Dcw6FwPhX/-1 of 1-/premium-uk/0 A1

Thank
you for
shopping
at
Amazon.co.uk!

Packing slip for
Your order of 14 January 2021
Order ID 203-0401178-9593158

Qty.	Item	Bin
1	**SMILE: A Modern Dictionary for Waiters** Paperback. Donatiello, Vincenzo. B08RH45355 : B08RH45355 : 9798584711207	

This shipment completes your order.
You can always check the status of your orders or change your account details from the "Your Account" link at the top of each page on our site.

Thinking of returning an item? PLEASE USE OUR ON-LINE RETURNS SUPPORT CENTRE.

Our Returns Support Centre (www.amazon.co.uk/returns-support) will guide you through our Returns
Policy and provide you with a printable personalised return label. Please have your order number ready (you
can find it next to your order summary, above). Our Returns Policy does not affect your statutory rights

0/Dcw6FwPhX/-1 of 1-//AMZL-DHP1-ND/premium-uk/0/0117-23:00/0117-07:49 Pack Type : A1

To my Family.
To the Waiters.

PREFACE

Speaking of hospitality, we almost always start from the incorrect assumption that there is a right and universal way to put people at ease. To be an artist of dining room service means to be able to pamper someone without them ever feeling the touch, to sew a tailored suit for each guest using sensations and caresses instead of fabric. Instead it is often interpreted as a rigid code to be followed to the letter even at the expense of making our poor customers suffer an unwelcome spectacle. When the desire for self-celebration exceeds the one of being at another's disposal, the service in a restaurant loses its sense of connection between the kitchen and the customer; it becomes unsolicited and, by definition, defies its intentions.

If, on the other hand, it is possible to discern the nuances of character and mood from the people who pass through a dining room, to enjoy the satisfaction of having made a guest feel content by meeting their expectations, exceeding them, the profession of waiter can make a human being feel complete and grateful like few other jobs in the world. It is a high point of empathy, a job that transforms you into an agent on a mission capable of capturing needs even before they are expressed or manifested, releasing adrenaline down your veins every time you manage to solve a social puzzle.

Vincenzo Donatiello is one of the great Italian interpreters of dining room service in the new millennium. A boy who grew up in compliance with the sacred classical rules and then knew how to emancipate himself; giving rise to his own service style based on malleability and on a new reading of daily situations. Because welcoming is first and foremost observation and analysis, Vincenzo did not write a manual or a book with the claim to teach others how it is in the world, he has simply given us a practical demonstration of service by providing a glossary of ideas and stories from which everyone can feel free to glean what is relevant to their own attitude, mood or situation.

As you read his lines, you can imagine him standing composed in the corner of the room smiling at you, at ease with the fact you are secure and comfortable until your next desire.

It is hospitality; a lifestyle much more than a job.

Enzo and Paolo Vizzari

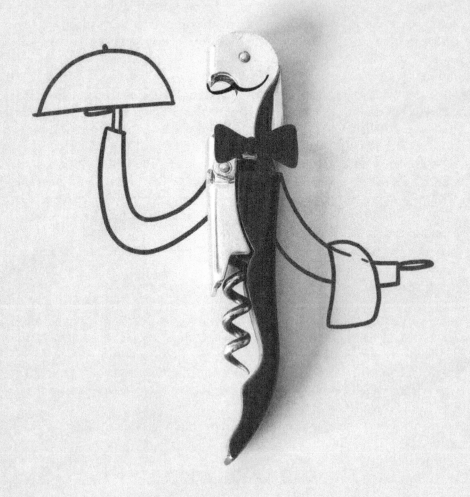

INTRODUCTION

I am a waiter.
Sometimes a psychologist.
A friend and confidant.
I can be a comedian when needed.
An ambassador of territories, near and far.
A gastronome.
I can become a babysitter, or even a dog-sitter.
You know I talk and tell so much but I actually listen even more.
I smile. Always.
Because I have chosen the best job in the world.

THE WAITER

A job that allows me to travel. Even standing still.
Every day, every single service is a discovery.
Every table, every guest.
Meetings of cultures.
Vitality.
Life.
This Work today is rich in intangible but essential elements.
Present and at the same time invisible.
As only the men and women of service know how to be.
I decided that the time was ripe for me to tell the everyday life of this Work.
How to do it?
What is the right idea?

THE WORDS.

So here comes
Smile - A Modern Dictionary for Waiters.
Enjoy the reading.

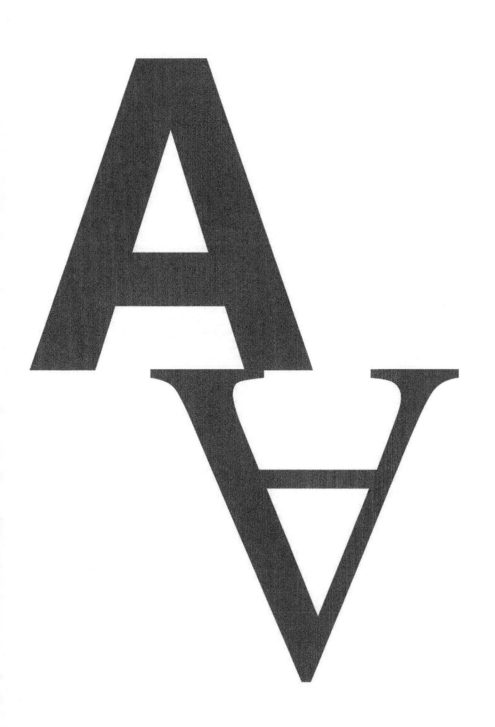

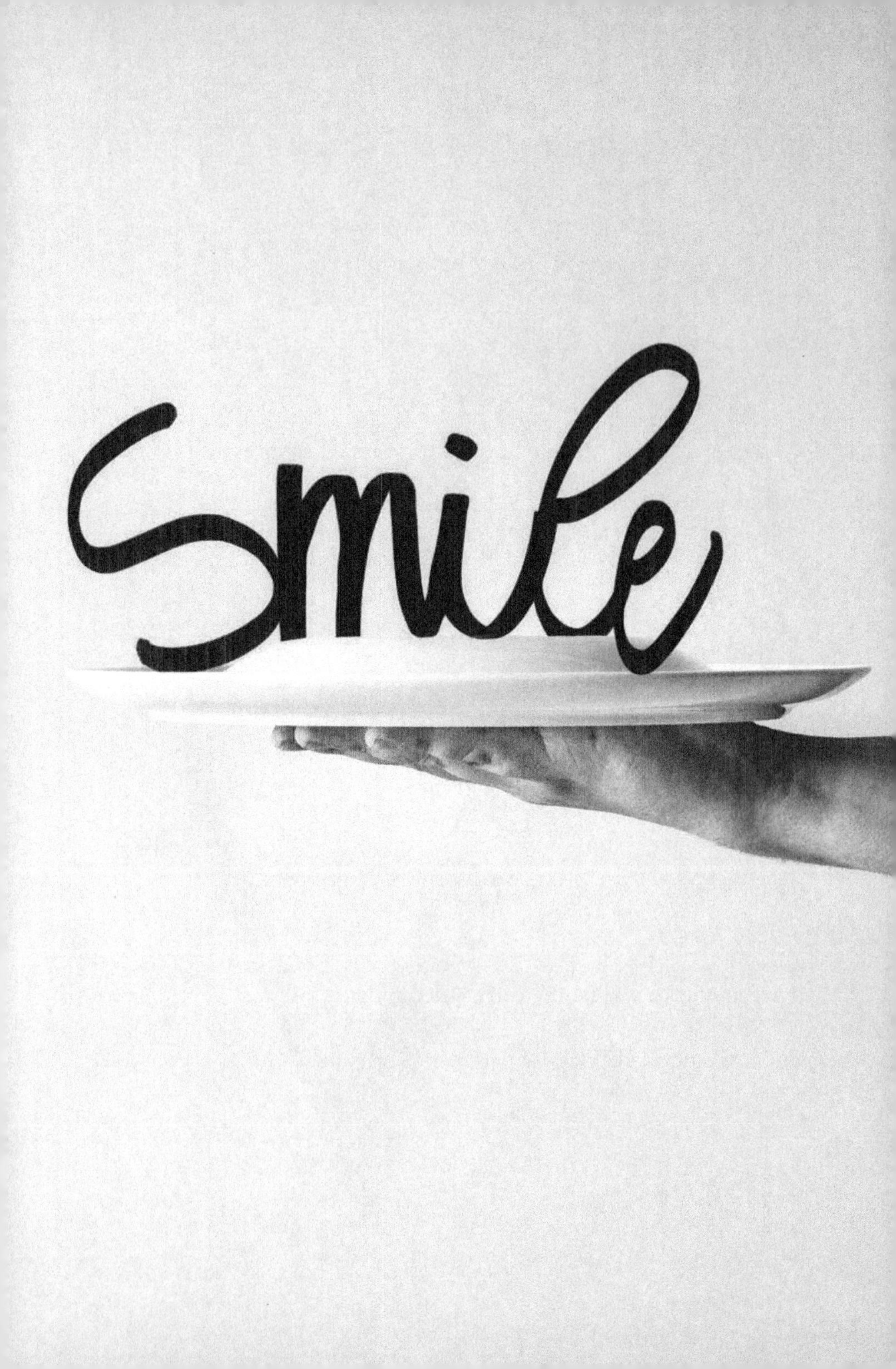
Smile

ACCOGLIENZA

I offer it to you first as it is our theme and should be held next to every other word in this dictionary as you consider their importance in the dining room.
In Italian accoglienza translates simply to...

HOSPITALITY

The magic word of our work. To welcome, to be able to welcome and to know how to welcome.

The human warmth of a sincere smile, or rather, of a smile that shows you at the first approach that they are there for you. All this is welcoming. The pleasure of feeling pampered and special, for just once or for a multitude of occasions.

Italy is the country of hospitality and its excellence. A heritage of men and women in the dining room who have made this concept great. There is no pre-established place for welcoming guests: from large private homes to luxury hotels, from guesthouses on the Riviera to gastronomic catering, from the village tavern to the Sport Bar, which awaits us in the morning for coffee and the football scores.

There is no pre-established place to welcome a guest. There are people who know how to make a place welcoming and they are the special people who, if we are lucky, will be the ones welcoming us.

Welcome is a sincere dialogue. Look whoever is in front of us in the eye and make him
understand that we are there for him, because it is important.

I was struck by a phrase from Pope Francis-

"Dialogue arises from an attitude of respect towards another person, from the belief that the other has something good to say; it presupposes making room, in our hearts, for his point of view, his opinion and his proposals. Dialogue means a cordial welcome and not a preventive condemnation. To dialogue, you need to know how to lower your defences, open the doors of your home and offer human warmth ".

ABILITIES

"Success is not final, failure is not fatal: it is the courage to continue that counts."
I didn't write this or say it, or at least I didn't say it first. It's a Sir Winston Churchill aphorism that I often use.

Success, failure and courage go hand in hand with abilities.

Each one of us has different abilities, which are used in different situations, in more or less-appropriate ways. Sometimes we do it better, others a little bit less. Certainly everyone has his own skills and everyone must, necessarily, understand what skills they possess.

Very often we forget it, but the fact of forgetting to use our abilities or silencing them, can be detrimental to our work, to the service that we owe to our guest, for the comfort and support that the brigade needs in order to do its best.

Let's say a team member is naturally inclined in empathising with the customer, always finding the right words, or another has flawless communication skills. Let's assume that another one is specialises in explaining the wines on the list and suppose that a third one has great care in welcoming our guests.

The restaurant manager's duty, and hence his ability, must be the one of giving each component in the brigade the rightful place, in the best possible context. Metaphorically, a perfect brigade is comparable to a puzzle: to obtain the whole picture, every piece needs to be placed in complementary way.

A good leader must be able to humbly understand his staff's innate abilities and to mix them in a perfect combination, in order to achieve an impeccable service unique to that team.

Even before that, with an eye to what combination of duties are required, a restaurant manager should scout his own talent.

ADRENALINE

Adrenaline. I say it again: adrenaline.

In our job we cannot do without it, we can easily affirm that adrenaline is indispensable to achieve a valuable result.

It is the petrol that ignites our engines and doesn't let you sleep at night, because even when you're home, after a day's work, it still runs through our veins.

Adrenaline is understanding what you are experiencing. You need to know which is the best way to use it, for and with others. Sometimes you're asked to handle one of your travel companion too, balancing and filling the gaps.
It needs to run in the room as a powerful flow of energy. Pre-service is like an athletic training: you stand in the pits, like a thoroughbred horse, pawing, waiting to gallop.

When you get to the end you will still feel the vibrations. You are not overloaded, it's just the way the things are.

Sometimes love and passion for this job are not enough. We need a small boost, the one that makes it even clearer there is only one goal: to give our best to this job. The adrenaline helps.

Synthesised, it is released into the circulation: it is a chemical reaction and, like all reactions, it creates.

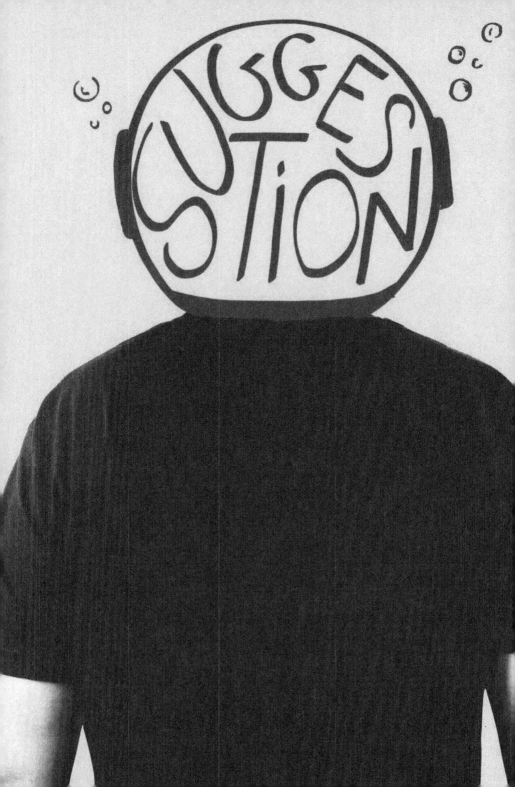

ADVICE

Advice: it spreads and expands like dry autumn leaves in a good breeze. But it is not to be underestimated because, although sometimes it can be annoying, it is imperative if our work is to be improved.

A customer who, with sensitivity, recommends changing some habits or reveals an innovation that was not previously in practice, is certainly to be appreciated.
Advice is always welcome.

Just as it is also important for a restaurant manager to advise the brigade on which tasks are to be performed.

The important thing is not to lose your temper and let words spring from the mind uncontrolled.

Advice should always be sought. It is what we do when we are not sure of something, hoping to receive confirmation of what we sometimes already know.

One day I asked a friend of mine why he went to the psychologist, he replied that it was comforting to expose a problem and then work through its precise meaning to an effective conclusion.
He then added that his therapist never really answered, he only supervised my friend as he gave himself the confirmation.

We often already know the answer, even when we wish not too.
When I am asked for advice, I wait a moment before giving an answer.
The advice must be always considered or it will not be valued.

William Shakespeare wrote: *"Everyone can master a grief but he that has it"*
Carefully chosen advice is a present, an act of kindness and when considered and offered in kindness it cannot fail to be constructive.

ATMOSPHERE

It is the air we breathe, that surrounds us, that creates the envelope around the room, the customer, the brigade.

It is never the same as it changes depending on mood, time, even perfumes ...
It can be light, crisp, pure or gloomy, heavy and suffocating.

In a dining room as in any other living space, the atmosphere is a balance between mood and climate: it is orchestral instruments well coordinated with each other to ensure that ineffable notes arise, a musicality that can blend a team's coordination with well-being of the guest who desires to be hosted by the fresh breeze of a smile, who cherishes a warm welcome or is comforted when hearing the right word ...

I always try to create the perfect ambience.

The ideal atmosphere allows the May rose to bloom silently, with much love, with a secret language that only a passionate heart can truly articulate .

Creating the right ambiance will be the key to your focus, take a deep breath, work peacefully and with the right concentration, offer the best you can do since we are all in the right place, at the right time.

ATTENTION

From the dictionary: the act of watching, listening or thinking about somebody or something carefully.
And so it is.

Attention is the act of giving, offering something to someone: a process that in the dining room, as in life, cannot fail. To turn your soul towards the customer, or a member of the team, is the way to make him feel less alone, just as if you were saying 'I'm here, I see you for who you are and am ready to take care of you with clear mind and thought'.

Attention is a thin, inner, intellectual feeling that touches emotional chords and cannot afford to be ignored since it is a faithful friend of hospitality.
Who could be unhappy and dissatisfied in the midst of lively, intense and curious attention?
Nobody.
Why?
Because each one of us needs another's attention, someone willing to listen and to give us an answer, a sign that makes us understand another's care will protect us.

To be attentive to a team member, understand and assist them to resolve their difficulties even with just a look, a pat on the back or a handful of words, can help to make an impeccable service; just as the opposite can be equally harmful, not only for your teammate, but for everyone, diners and waiters.

I believe that society is well served when you can be sure to lean on each other, lovingly, without fear and without judgement.

The same has to do with a customer who, if pampered with the right dose of care, obviously without exceeding social niceties, would regard his experience as stimulating, welcoming and above all deserving of being repeated.

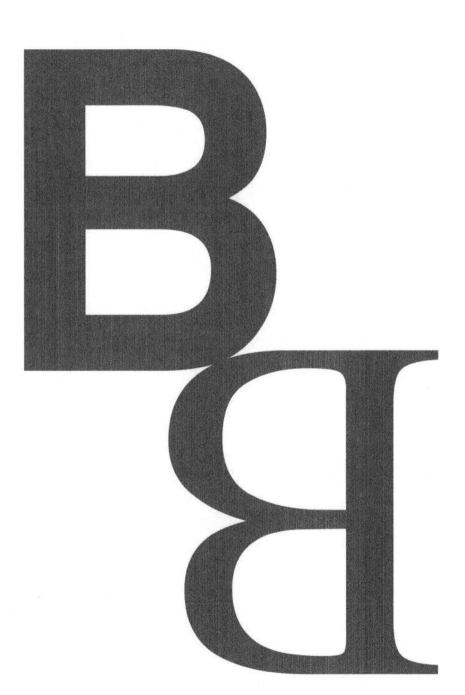

BEAUTY

Lovely, attractive, giving pleasure to the senses; from Old French beaute, based on Latin bellus.

The etymology of the adjective we are analysing is emblematic because it catches the eye as a very simple and easy word, sometimes even trivialised, but it hides a difficult and slippery concept.

Poets in every time and place have written verse that no-one else dared because they were trying to capture either the simplest or the most complicated way to describe beauty; sometimes both.

"And I'll tell you for what secret, the hills on clear horizons
they curve like lips that a prohibition close, and because the will to say
make them beautiful, beyond any human desire
Yes it seems, may the soul love them every evening
of stronger love ".

An example above all is the poet Gabriele D'Annunzio: although he loved to play with the dictionary, looking for words that are sometimes very difficult and obsolete, in his poem "Sera fiesolana" he finds no better word to describe the gentle shapes of the hills on the horizon....." e perché la volontà di dire le faccia belle"

Rough translation- "and because the will to say makes them beautiful"

Which word could be indeed more intense and immediate than the adjective "beautiful"?

Everyone understands the aesthetic but still wonders what the true meaning of beauty is.

Fyodor Dostoevsky wrote in The Idiot: - *"Beauty will save the world".*

And therefore, beyond any etymology, even in our service beauty makes the difference.

The beauty of a sincere welcome, the beauty in the ambience, the beauty of people, the beauty of customers, the beauty of conviviality. That's it: to breathe and yearn for the deepest beauty.

It is necessary to simplify the notion in order for it to be useful to us: beauty is already banal in itself and that's exactly why it's very hard to deal with, it is necessary to claim it with all one's strength. Do not forget: while the most beautifully simple path will sometimes be the correct choice, it will always give us deep emotions.

Come to think of it I take back the title of my book 'I serve' and rename it:
'I serve beauty, and I like it!'

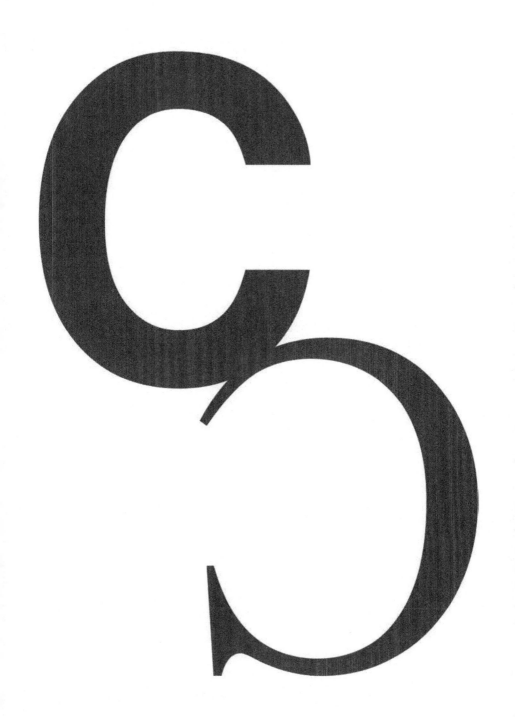

CALM

"Keep calm and carry on" - it's on everything from t-shirts to coffee mugs.

This is the imperative used by every parent: "You need to calm down!". When you are young you take this as boring advice: you don't understand why serenity is so important, like the piece of a puzzle without which the game could not be completed. Then you grow up, you begin to stumble upon the world of work and understand that yes, calm is essential for you and for others.

A service carried out with great care and tranquility will always appear more eloquent and because you complete your duties with professional poise they will be received with a higher appreciation.

Latins used to say "Virtus placidi fortis est" and it is more or less as the English idiom "Calmness belongs to the strong".

A couple of hyper-known phrases, the ones that get into your head, but you don't really understand.
I didn't understand it immediately either, I discovered it over the years.
Sometimes getting old is necessary …

There is no need to panic, to lose your temper, it is useless. Rather better think about how to keep a cool head.

Calm is not a facade, because the customer would notice it, this is the concept you must well express to your team: calm cannot be improvised.

"Take your time among noises and haste, and remember how peaceful could be the silence" - Annon.

CARE

"I'll protect you from the fears of hypochondria
From the disturbances that from today you will encounter on your way
From the injustices and deceptions of your time
From the failures that by your nature you will normally attract
I will relieve you of your pains and mood swings
From the obsessions of your manias
I will overcome the gravitational currents
Space and light to keep you from getting old ... "

When I think of Care, I think of Franco Battiato.

The first two stanzas perfectly summarise what, in plain English, would be indefinable.

Care is intangible because it is weightless. Pure care is the act of taking care, both taken and given by oneself to another. Forgive the turn of phrase, these songwriters are poets at heart.

In the dining room it is affection for the customer, it is the clearest and most credible cuddle that can be offered, it is being next to him, making him feel the gentleness of another, the human warmth, to heal him from the stress of the world, stop the frenzy, open our heart so that his will also expand.

CAREER

Have you ever tried to type the word career into an online search engine? I just did it. I tried a lot of them. Career in Wikipedia. Career in Treccani Encyclopaedia. Your career. On-line career services.
Career is the personal path of an individual in working and/or professional life.
Career plan of the University of ...
Make a career in that or that company ...

Career related searches: career meaning, career synonym, career etymology, career in English, make a career, career adjectives, advance career ...
Ok, you get the point. My aim is not to bore you but to illustrate the varied meaning of the term. It differs for everyone.

Career for me is making a life path, improving yourself, reaching goals that you have set along the way, and as a result of your effort, believing in what you do.
I believe aiming for the top is, physiologically, a way to feel that you have found your place in the world.
Career is sweat, commitment, tenacity, a drive to never give up, in other words: a great career is the result of honest hard work while doing what you love.

Especially in this context it is important to understand that the idea of service is at the heart of my analysis. In order to do a great job, we need to know how to serve, by doing this well we will reach our goals. We will, on a personal level, get more and more from ourselves.
I like to summarise in this way, with the help of Nelson Mandela, when he said: "Don't judge me for my successes but for all those times I've fallen and managed to get up".
In this job, like a thousand others, as always, we slip, fall, get up. It is called strength. It's called perseverance. It's called sheer bloody mindedness. It's progress.

It's called a career.

24

CLEANLINESS

A while ago a sentence struck me.
The only problem is that I don't remember who wrote it, in any case I read it on Twitter.

It sounded more or less like this: *"Instead of cleaning the house, I'm in charge of logistical dust management."*

Apart from dust, or maybe not, we can also speak of the dust; but we must speak of logistics.

Cleaning is organisation.
It is essential, especially in a job that includes the serving of food and drink.
Eating on a dirty floor or in a cluttered environment is inconceivable.
Even more annoying is when the bathroom is indecent, customers are allowed to see the toilets. Imagine what they think of the kitchen if your bathroom is dirty!

It is good manners to wash your hands before sitting at the table, so frequenting an environment that emits a cacophony of odours certainly doesn't make your mouth water.

Cleaning is order.

An untidy or cluttered environment will not make the customer or staff concentrate. In the chaos there is a risk of catastrophe, as if we put a thousand post-it notes on a fifteenth-century fresco.
The overall picture would be messy and disfigured of its essence.

During a sketch, the Italian comedian Gabriele Cirilli, dealing with household chores, said-
"My wife is a clean freak. Kills microbes one by one, she knows them all by name".
I would like to be his wife.

COMMITMENT

You can never have enough.

Sometimes we are ferocious with ourselves, we feel as though we have been asked too much. This involves one immense effort to overcome the desire to give up, to keep going ...
Without commitment, dedication, you will not climb the mountain and the view isn't as majestic if the climb was too easy.

Martin Luther King wrote, in this regard:

"If you can't be a pine on the top of the hill,
Be a scrub in the valley...but be
The best little scrub by the side of the rill;
Be a bush if you can't be a tree.
If you can't be a bush, be a bit of the grass,
And some highway happier make.
If you can't be a highway, then just be a trail,
If you can't be a sun, be a star.
We can't all be captains, we've got to be crew.
There's something for all of us here.
It isn't by size that you win or you fail...
Be the best of whatever you are!"

If fate dealt has offered us this work, hospitality, it means that it is now part of our being. The customer demands commitment, we must do the same.
Commitment to understand each other so that the service is impeccable.

Commitment is to understand that climbing is tiring.
Commitment is to believe in the diners, in the team.
Commitment is knowing that yes, you can rely on yourself.
Commitment is to overcome every tremor and reach the euphoria of beauty for the little things.

COMMON SENSE

This stranger.

Joking aside, I often remind myself that in all situations it is necessary to use common sense, every circumstance is good as long as it is sustainable. Common sense is a factual situation and, at the same time, a way.

Let's imagine a situation of unease among the members of the brigade. Let's think again about a qui pro quo with a client. Billions of situations come to mind in which everything seemed to crack, yet when you play the common sense card it seems that everything returns to a balance.

The myriad of times in which we have heard the phrase "it's just common sense!" Seems disproportionate with the sentiment being described. It seemed obvious in retrospect, superfluous, almost cliché.
But no. There is the truth in its naivety.

The time has now come to ask ourselves what this 'common' sense is. Above all what common sense is in the room.

Common sense is the ability to reasonably judge a situation and discern the practical needs that it entails. Common sense is to use all our physical and mental capacity with the addition of a component of sweetness to resolve uncomfortable situations with fairness and empathy.

It is amazing how when one uses the correct tone of voice, gesture and words, always with the addition of common sense, it leads to amazing results: happy staff, satisfied customers and a general air of welcome.

Common sense is a way of life that is unfortunately far too uncommon.

COMMUNICATION

There are plenty of blogs that teach what communication is, how it goes applied and what are the rules for it to be effective and to directly touch one's interlocutor mind and heart.
Well, in a restaurant, communication is sacred.

There are some ingredients that cannot be missing in the relationship between the actors: the dining room staff, the restaurant manager, the kitchen brigade and, last but not least, the customer.

It makes no difference who you are talking to, if it is to the colleague or to the customer who's waiting for your explanations, what really matters is that you know how to mix and dose the elements of engaging communication.

Which are those elements?

First of all, we must be conscious of the situation in which we find ourselves, never forgetting that every service is different, every day carries along a subtly new scene and a new approach to compliment it.

Secondly, it is necessary to create empathy, knowing how to listen, paying attention to any need while observing the smallest details all the while seasoning the intercourse with a a good dose of assertiveness and a pinch of creativity for good measure.

Communication is the basis of a relationship, a good society works when everyone feels free to communicate with those around him because he has the skills to do it right, or has learned how to do it well. If he cannot excel with talent, he tries with commitment, because as communicating can be a gift, it can also be learned.

Lastly, what is meant by a good communicator? You will be a good communicator when you will be able to enter the hearts of those in front of you and satisfy their needs.

CONTACT

"I know how you feel... It's like being behind glass, you can't touch anything you see. I spent three quarters of my life locked out, until I realised that the only way is to break it. And if you are afraid of getting hurt, try to imagine that you are already old and almost dead, full of regrets" reveals the writer Andrea De Carlo.

We say contact but could just as easily say touch, in a professional relationship this can be tricky. When you interact with a person in a social environment like a restaurant it is easy to go too far into their personal space and make the person uncomfortable, for a new customer a handshake and a sincere smile are perfect. Even with regular guests a reserved approach is seen as professional and kind, nothing more until initiated by the custo-mer.

When in doubt it is better to behave formally than be too familiar.

In rare cases a warm hug works well with an affectionate guest, with whom we have already established a good relationship, and it feels good too.

For a member of our brigade, who needs support, the pat on the back is perfect, the classic one that makes you understand that you are there and you will support him whatever happens.

Usually, in our own private life, we should refer to William Shakespeare's words -

"Look how he rests his cheek on that hand! Oh, if I were a glove over his hand, to be able to touch that cheek!"

CONVERSATION

Conversation is a way of understanding the other, understanding what they are thinking.

Conversation is breathing in deeply.

The writer Fabrizio Caramagna highlighted - *"In the midst of so much chatter, banality and insignificant sounds, there are few true words we exchange every day. Maybe we fall in love in order to really start talking"*

Service is a form of falling in love. Conversation in service is the culmination of a marriage that radiates truth and love.
What is nicer than to speak and to listen? We must endeavour to choose the best register to tend to the heart of those who are listening to us.

Conversing is more than tea and pastries.

Conversing is a silky kiss that leaves its mark.

CORDIALITY

World Kindness Day is celebrated on 13 November.
In fact, this date was the opening day of the "World Kindness Movement" conference held in Tokyo in 1997 and concluded with the signing of the 'Declaration of Kindness'.

But this is just a note, because we will talk about kindness later. Now we are talking about cordiality, which is not only for the guests: it is a human friendliness that can be summed up as such:

People who show cordiality are polite, kind, and pleasant, but the word implies a bit of reserve: you might appreciate the cordiality among the employees at your job, but your relationships with your closest friends and family are characterised by an emotion deeper than cordiality.

Being cordial as a waiter means adopting behaviours that are as affable and kind as they are captivating and capable of capturing the attention of the other which, in this case, can be understood as the customer or a colleague but always keeping a professional demeanour.

Being cordial is not just trying to be nice, it is a way of being ourselves by offering the best of what we can do to another in a polite way. The manifestation of our interest will not always be the same, there are days when we will feel better and others when we would just like to put our heads under the earth exactly like ostriches do. Yet there are ways of training oneself to be more cordial in professional situations.

Entering into the perspective that we can truly be good with ourselves and with others, without caring too much about the negative sides that work offers us, then we will be impeccable and cordial servants.

Cordiality is at the core of hospitality.
Cordiality is leaving the best memory of us impressed in the customer's mind because, whenever he returns, he will be happy to see us.

COURTESY

Text from the dictionary:

"Courtesy is a complex of qualities, including, respect towards others, benevolence towards inferiors, pleasantness of conversation, disdain of all cowardice, and defence of the oppressed and of women, which, in the chivalric education of the Middle Ages, constituted an important characteristic of the court man".

Although this list seems varied there is a common thread no?

That courtesy is infinite. Everything is in it, from chivalrous love, to courtesy between people and for the guest.

It is a way of welcoming those in front of us without restrictions or unnecessary frills.

It is the mirror of the soul.

CRITICISM

Criticism should be constructive. I start using this condition because, alas, many times, it isn't.

When a criticism is made, I have learned, before taking it personally one should ponder whether this is founded. If it is, then almost always it can be accepted as advice which is a positive rather than criticism which can be seen as negative.

When people are just being critical I like to recall a line from Charlie Chaplin-

"They will always criticise you, they will speak ill of you and it will be difficult for you to meet anyone to who likes you for who you are!
So live, do what your heart tells you!
Life is like a play that has no rehearsal:
Sing.
Dance.
Laugh.
Live intensely every day of your life before the opera ends without applause"

Criticism must create an improvement: to those who like to criticise without foundation I say that it is useless to spend our lives avoiding criticism that, even before being made to others, they are made to ourselves.

We should look good in our boots, to get to know each other thoroughly and avoid criticising others.

Then I think that grandparents proverb that rings true more than any other as they often do-

"Before judging anyone, walk a mile in the their shoes ".

CUDDLE

A sweet squeeze of the cheek by grandmother before sitting for the Sunday lunch is a good example.

Yet, behind this cuddly noun, there is a world to dissect, mould into something our own , to offer as a gift.

The cuddle lies in falling asleep under a padded and perfumed duvet when it rains outside, it is to taste the sweet and frothy cream of the profiteroles, it's an unexpected kiss, a warm hug, a relaxing massage ...
Is that it?
Nope, it's more, much more.

A cuddle is an external gesture that makes our eyes light up, warms the heart and sometimes brings butterflies into the stomach.
Receiving a cuddle is feeling loved, offering a cuddle is loving.

How is pampering in the service portrayed?
It is dictated by two factors: the passion for one's work, which in itself is not enough, and that intense love that we feel, every day, that we feel when we offer a caress to our client in the right dose, paying attention to his being, perceiving what he seeks and how he wants to be pampered. An encore of a dish that he particularly liked, a glass of wine he has never tasted before, a smile, may be enough...

Finally, sincere gratitude for being able to serve him. This is not just a profession, it is a way of life: empathy in making the customer understand that we are at his complete disposal because we love to do it, and we wouldn't want to be anywhere else but at his table.

I think this is the most beautiful, immense and elegant demonstration that can be given to him.
Nothing else is needed. No other words or commas are needed to explain.

Cuddling is the charm that creates alchemy and grace.

CULTURE

One of my dear friends was whilst a student, was told told her that: *"Culture is not eaten but it helps not to be eaten."*

It makes much more sense in Italian but the gist of the saying is that while we don't need Culture to survive it helps us to be better if we can continue to develop good ideas from others while learning from their mistakes. For example - building fortified walls to keep out predators. If, god forbid, there was a cataclysmic event that took away most of our population, most of the skills we take for granted would be lost, we would be inside this problem learning every basic need from scratch.
That's an example of lost culture at its most brutal.

In a more practical case we must understand every facet of our culture: environmental knowledge handed down through generations, traditions of our territory, of folklore and human evolution, of intellectual progress, and probably most relevant, our culinary and enological heritage. It is also to know the best way of dealing with the rest of the world, each has its own customs and beliefs.

It is not enough to mnemonically learn historical events as taught in school -

"In fourteen hundred ninety-two
Columbus sailed the ocean blue.

He had three ships and left from Spain;
He sailed through sunshine, wind and rain."
....and so on.
It works to remember dates but there is no understanding of time and place.

Culture is also that which is discovered by listening to the stories of the elderly, observing one's mother, stopping for a few moments to observe sections of the world that offer infinite spectacles.

My favourite is the culture of food, wine and service.

"I think food, culture, people and landscape are all absolutely inseparable." - Anthony Bourdain

Sometimes it happened that some people have commented, dealing with my free time, that I traveled a lot or have had exaggerated experiences in Italy or abroad for wineries and restaurants.

First of all it is a way to occupy the periods of time in which I am not working, therefore a passion.

Secondly it is a way to acculturate myself and increase knowledge to be always ready and capable in a world that is anything but consistent. I urge everyone to travel more and eat everything they find there.

CUSTOMER

It is curious how, in ancient Rome, the customer was the citizen who accepted the protection of an authoritative, influential person in exchange for generic services, especially in the sphere of civil and political life.
Today, the customer, our customer, is the one who benefits from our service and, in the circumstances, invests, actually I misspoke: he pays.

Is the customer always right? Well lets just say the customer is never wrong, there's a difference...

The customer is the pinnacle of our work, we have a commitment of service that will cost a great deal of dedication and special attention. Establishing equality between customers, dedicating them the same time or perceiving what their individual needs are, is an essential step in satisfying them and fully responding to their needs.

When does a customer feel in the right place at the right time?
When he is amazed. In a positive way of course.

Although some circumstances are not born as rosy, the room manager and his brigade must be ready, attentive, they must show a great ability to improvise and bring some not inconsiderable psychological skill to the table, the careful goal to bring their customer back to a state of calm.

We ourselves are the customer.
Thinking as a customer, and not as a waiter, during service will allow us to change the view and find an ease of communication with different groups in a short period of time.

The old adage *"treat people how you would like to be treated"* is useful to remember here.

There is no service without a customer.
There is no customer without service.

CUSTOMS AND TRADITIONS

It is curious how, in ancient Rome, the customer was the citizen who accepted the protection of an authoritative, influential person in exchange for generic services, especially in the sphere of civil and political life. Today, the customer, our customer, is the one who benefits from our service and, in the circumstances, invests, actually I misspoke: he pays.

Is the customer always right? Well lets just say the customer is never wrong, there's a difference…

The customer is the pinnacle of our work, we have a commitment of service that will cost a great deal of dedication and special attention. Establishing equality between customers, dedicating them the same time or perceiving what their individual needs are, is an essential step in satisfying them and fully responding to their needs.

When does a customer feel in the right place at the right time? When he is amazed. In a positive way of course.

Although some circumstances are not born as rosy, the room manager and his brigade must be ready, attentive, they must show a great ability to improvise and bring some not inconsiderable psychological skill to the table, the careful goal to bring their customer back to a state of calm.

We ourselves are the customer.
Thinking as a customer, and not as a waiter, during service will allow us to change the view and find an ease of communication with different groups in a short period of time.

The old adage *"treat people how you would like to be treated"* is useful to remember here.

There is no service without a customer.
There is no customer without service.

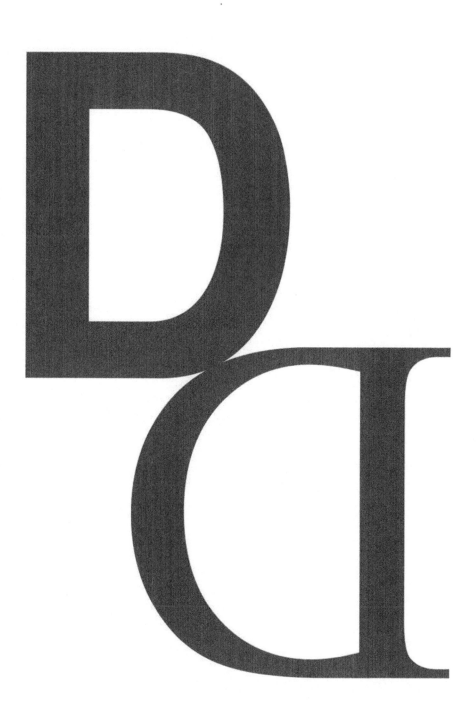

DEDICATION

Dedication is when you give your all for something, when you infuse your energy fully to be able to give your best.

"More important are total dedication and a tendency to underestimate difficulties which cause one to tackle problems that other, more critical and acute persons, choose to avoid" said Rita Levi-Montalcini.

Being a success in the restaurant industry takes dedication. For those who succeed is (usually) a welcome distraction from everyday life. Somewhere the results of hard work and progress are evident every minute of every day.

When the heart and mind are activated to ensure that the experience is optimum, then of course, we will be totally dedicated to our customers. There is no solution: without love, passion and dedication we would not be able to empathise in the correct way.

Any job in contact with people that is done well requires presence of mind and a dedication to excellence, in owning the role, in responding cordially with a smile, in making them perceive that we are present, that we are doing our best, that we have been chosen for this job because that's right, we know how to do it ... with dedication.

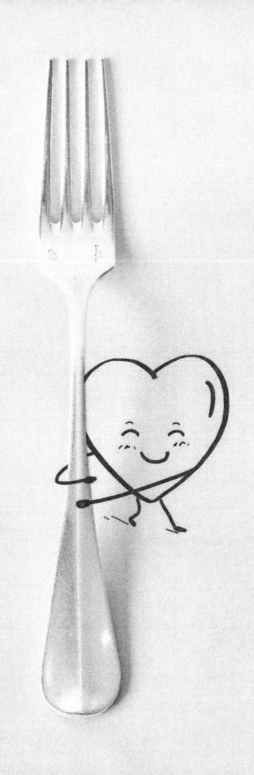

DETAILS

Details are important. We all know this, we say it all the time;

"the devil's in the detail"

Most commonly attributed to Friedrich Wilhelm Nietzsche, the German philosopher and poet.
He was quoted as saying *"Der Teufel stecktim Detail"* which translates to *"the devil is in the details."*
Almost definitely a corruption of fellow German, Gustave Flaubert's original quote
"God is in the details." - a fair point considering Flaubert was an architect, and a distinction we can carry over to the dining room.

Nietzshe almost certainly had a practical purpose in mind, as a philosopher, and also the lesson we can loosely translate to- The details of a plan, while seeming insignificant, may contain hidden problems that threaten its overall feasibility.

Also very true in a restaurant.

The details for a mise en place, for an outfit, for the perfect manners, for a perfect hospitality.

I say it again: details are important.
The detail is a minutia, but it cannot be overlooked, in any way.

During the service the details are gigantic, because, if not respected, they will be immediately noticed.
It makes no difference whether it is a starred restaurant, a tavern, a trattoria or a food truck, the details must be taken care of.

Sometimes I think to pay so much attention to the details is a form of compulsive mania, yet I must admit they can make a big difference.

Imagine a perfectly set table: the white tablecloth, all arranged in the best possible way and... a stain!
A small blemish on perfection.
Rest assured: it will be noticed immediately and you will be reprimanded for that minutia if noticed by a manager and thought of poorly if noticed by a customer first.

Just a detail? Maybe, but a detail left out.
Be the perfect detail yourself, the rest will follow.

DIALOGUE

What is the essential condition of engaging dialogue? To converse respectfully is to put yourself in the other's shoes, to wear his trousers.

Dialogue means acknowledging the other and starting from the belief that what he is about to tell us makes sense to him.

Dialogue is listening without judgement.

"I don't have to agree with you to like you or respect you." - Anthony Bourdain

We must lower our defences in front of the customer because it is precisely the ability to let go of our own ego that will allow us to accept the others opinion.

Everyone will receive a compliment from customers or colleagues from time to time, as well as disappointment and criticism: if you understand them as constructive and useful, without immediately behaving defensively, then you will "make room" for opinions and proposals, you will open a dialogue that can lead to a lesson worth learning.
Or not worth anything, that is the way it works. You must be open to all.

Opening your mind to dialogue is opening your heart to other opinions that you may learn from.

DINING ROOM

Perhaps the emblem of the whole book, this place is definitely the setting.

A dining room or lounge is ideally a large, comfortable, bright place where you are most at home with your loved ones, both in private and in public.

In Italy we refer the restaurant dining room the 'Sala' - simply the 'Room'.

The Room is a place. Material. The Room is a concept. Immaterial.

We are all men and women of the dining room, we serve by definition, no ifs, no buts, we always believe in the best for the customer.

The room is a warm welcome place.
It has to be clean, the service has to be attentive, and people have to be comfortable.

There must be no room for unnecessary frills, nothing that doesn't add something, pointless embellishment for the sake of it would kill the ambience. Much like on a plate of food.

The room is tidy, precise, in the room everyone knows what to do, where to go and what his mission is.

The dining room must become the home of customers and waiters: it is like an exotic aquarium that instills passion in both diner and waiter alike.

Without the room there would be no customers and no workers to enjoy it.

The room is a vessel that holds our emotions, passions, motivations and the will to live, to live an intense life in full peace of mind because, as long as we are here, we will be in our perfect dimension.

DISCIPLINE

Some are born disciplined, many will be disciplined by the world.
Yet it is a constant for being talented at work.

Some believe order and preparation is a boulder to carry, others understand it is obvious.
The confusion is in how you have been disciplined.

I can only rely on experience.
I thank my first restaurant manager, who appears several times, for the immense effort he made me do it at the beginning of the profession, because discipline is learned in the field, you learn it by working and experimenting, it is not something in itself, it is the essence of the service so far.

"A disciplined mind leads to happiness, and an undisciplined mind leads to suffering",
argued the Dalai Lama.

In the mind of a man dedicated to discipline you will find purity of soul and spirit, his thoughts are not soiled or worn out by rottenness, and his life will always offer the best.

The service is good if accompanied by a good dose of discipline.

DISCOMFORT

You sweat. Yes, you read that correctly.
Discomfort brings sweat, because it hinders you.
What is it caused by?
Discomfort is a form of inadequacy with respect to the surrounding environment. There may be a more intense form of distress, personal or social distress, to be explored on a psychological level. Then there is the momentary discomfort, created by an uncomfortable situation.

Here, in this work it happens often.
Here, in this work it is strictly forbidden show you are suffering.

"It is a well understood truth in the hospitality industry, unlike almost every other profession, showing pain is a sign of weakness. If you don't believe me go work in any commercial kitchen for a week." - Marco Pierre White

Circumstances can be severe, but they cannot be overwhelming.
Making us fickle to discomfort won't get us far.

Here you need firm nerves, strong hearts and clear minds.

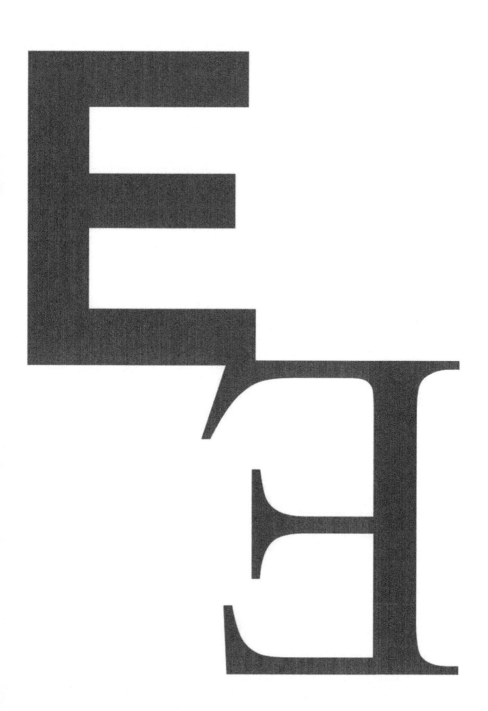

EASY

Nothing is easy: or everything is, it all depends on one's inclinations.

The old adage - *"Is your glass half full or half empty"* - the answer lies in your attitude.

Easy. It's also very personal, it's something that we do particularly well, that doesn't need a huge effort to be made. This relates to our unique skillset as much as the difficulty of the task at hand.

Sometimes easy is something we like, doing a task you enjoy is always easier than one you hate., at times we hate it because it inhibits our strength, it annihilates our own ego.

1 + 1 = 2. Amazing.
Yet there is also "2 + 2 is not always 4".
That's life.

Nothing is easy, nothing is impossible. But there is the talent to do something, bash some heads: what is easy is very difficult, do anything that at first glance seems impossible: here is the genius, that's all.
If it sounds easy, it's tough. If it seems difficult, it is impossible.

It's all in the way you approach the issue; with confidence for something you love and there is literally nothing that doesn't seem easy, even the difficult things are lightened with passion for the task.

"This ain't no tall order, this is nothing to me. Difficult takes a day, impossible takes a week."- Jay Z
Easy is often very complicated and there is nothing so easy that it becomes impractical when you do something unwillingly.
In this book, when you will reach the definition of zero, you will find there are zero mornings when I wake up without the desire to go to work.
My job is sometimes insurmountable, it almost seems like a mountain.
But it's easy, because I like it more than anything else in the world.

EFFICIENCY

I often wonder what's the difference between being efficient and being effective.

Being effective is based on how well you performed a task or illustrated a point of view. Efficiency signifies a level of performance that uses the least amount of inputs to achieve the highest amount of output. It minimises the waste of resources such as physical materials, energy, and time while accomplishing the desired output.

It practical terms it is the cheapest and easiest way to achieve the desired result, and who doesn't want that!

I like to think in this job efficiency goes hand in hand with effectiveness in fulfilling what is best at that exact moment because, as we said, it is important to do the right thing in the dining room of a restaurant, with care and efficiency of movement.

Only by focusing on essentiality can the time spent in carrying out any operation be reduced and we will have a clearer view of reality.

Efficiency should be combined with an energy that allows us to make the most of our talents, whatever they are: whoever is called to be a teacher should be the best teacher in the world, a chef should cook in the best way there is to cook, a musician should compose as if he were the greatest one in the universe, and so on.
An excellent performance of the brigade will lead to customer satisfaction as well as a less exhausted crew.

Efficiency is doing useful and beautiful things the most timely and graceful way.

ELEGANCE

Coco Chanel was one of the most important protagonists in twentieth century fashion. She was revolutionary not only for the ability to dress women, but also for the influence it had on their way of thinking.
I delighted in looking for some of the more famous quotes by Coco, there are many, all extremely graceful and refined.

"Elegance is when the inside is as beautiful as the outside."

"Simplicity is the key note of all elegance."

"The best things in life are free, the second best are very, very expensive."

"When I find a darker colour than black, I'll wear it. But until that time, I will wear black."

If we talk about elegance, we cannot miss to talk about restaurant uniforms
By that I mean that each will choose the most suitable one, not necessarily black, not necessarily luxurious.
What matters is the uniform is elegant.

Elegance can mean practical and functional, but also sober.

Elegance is about manners, it is the opposite of vulgarity.

Elegance is paying attention to details, it is the care of material and immaterial things.

Elegance is a way of being, a state of mind.

It is a gentle, delicate, graceful, pleasant and simple soul.

"Elegance is the art if not being astonishing" - Jean Cocteau

EMPATHY

It means reading the guest's wishes, anticipating questions, learning to see with the heart.

Professional empathy is learned by observing, by 'feeling' your way in situations.
Being in things, not above and not below.

Empathy is the ability to fully understand the state of mind of others, whether it is joy or pain. It is feeling the warmth of those who are working with you, of those you observe in order to serve them better.
From the very first moments, exactly when the customer crosses the threshold of your restaurant, you must be able to understand what his likes and dislikes are, to judge the the state of his mood at all times.

If you learn how the people around you prefer to be looked after then you will be perfectly tuned to their needs and perceive the smallest adjustments needed faster than if you are unaware of them.

You will need the right atmosphere, the strength to move forward, the ability to judge, to understand customs and traditions, common sense and, perhaps, etiquette. But empathy rules, it is the way to touch the emotional chords of those whom you relate to.

Empathy is being in others' shoes, putting on their boots and going for a walk.

"I'm not looking for absolution
Forgiveness for the things I do
But before you come to any conclusions
Try walking in my shoes" - Depeche Mode

ENERGY

Power! It seems to be the classic slogan for being amped up during sports.

TV commercials offer us a multitude of dietary supplements to increase our energy:

"Redbull gives you wings!"

Useful yes but unfortunately, if over consumed, Redbull is more likely to give you diabetes or liver disease before you sprout feathers and fly to the heavens.
Alas there is no magic ingredient that can offer our body the answer to a late night more than a balanced diet (and perhaps a strong cup of coffee).

You have energy inside, it is something that is created and generated by an alchemy between passion and endorphins. Energy is a state of mind that men and women in the dining room must have. Good health is a must for a constitution, a fact that is in direct opposition to most industry lifestyles and so why this is so important to uphold.
Healthy body, healthy mind.

And so our physical appearance can be flawless, yet without a good dose of energy in the mind we could not perform our duties.
I went in search of an aphorism that could identify what good room energy means, the one that does not lead to competition but to cooperation, the one that is released as if it were an explosion of colours that brighten people's faces and suddenly instil good mood. The energy that allows you to run, rather than walk.

"Every man and every woman is connected with the energy that many call "love", but which is actually the raw material with which the universe was created. This energy cannot be manipulated, it is it that gently guides us, it is in it that all our apprentice-ship for life is concentrated. If we try to direct it towards goals chosen by us, we end up at the mercy of despair, frustration, illusion, because it is free and wild "-
Paulo Coelho.

EQUALITY

It is a principle.

It is the basis of this work: between the manager and the other waiters, between client and client. Between us and our guests.

There can be no differences, no favouritism, you have to spend the same time., same energy, same attitude.

Too often service bends to the customer depending on a personal connection or we don't use the same attitude with everyone because we ourselves are moody.

Equality and respect, pampering every situation because it matters to us, we believe it.

Equality in the management of a dining room service is what helps us to be impeccable, we know this.

Every moment we must remember that we do not save lives, but we do strive to improve them and it will be pleasant, even joyous, but ultimately it will be a steady and unbiased service in beautiful surroundings that will make the difference. To everyone equally.

And the difference well made to all.

ETIQUETTE

Ok, let's go back to basics.

When was the etiquette born?

Given that the etiquette encompasses all the rules and good habits that each person should follow in various public situations, be they particular moments in life (weddings, parties or funerals), or more common situations, such as dinners in a restaurant, meetings with a friend, travel, gifts, job interviews, first dates. The lists of acceptable behaviour are as varied as the cultures and nationalities who invented them, and so the birth of etiquette is tricky to nail down.

The word Etiquette has its origin at French royal courts in the 1600s and 1700s. Etiquette used to mean "keep off the grass." When Louis IX's gardener at Versailles discovered that the aristocrats were trampling through his garden, he put up signs, or "etiquets," to warn them off, but the dukes and duchesses walked right past the signs. Finally, the king himself had to decree that no one was to go beyond the bounds of the etiquets. Gradually, the meaning of etiquette was expanded to include the ticket to court functions that listed the rules of where to stand and what to do. Like language, etiquette evolved, but in a sense it still means "keep off the grass." We watch for people to stay within certain bounds.

Yet the first written work of acceptable behaviour, especially table manners, is by the Italian Monsignor Giovanni Della Casa, almost 100 years earlier,
Dalla Casa's etiquette was published in 1558, and entitled *'Il Galateo overo de' costumi'*.

It is a real treatise that has a form on the style of a platonic dialogue carried out between the author himself and the young nephew Hannibal, the monsignor speaks of good manners, the previously unwritten rules on behaviour and customs that a man of his class had to follow. Everything that has been learned from a diplomat and man of the Church of the sixteenth century is passed on to the children.

61

The point is that there is no basic distinction between etiquette then and that of today: it is constantly a form of cordiality that must be fulfilled and carried forward, and it is not a matter of social class or of extraction, there are the unique, true and impeccable manners, which will make you a gentlemen, always.

'manners maketh man' - William Horman (1519) Headmaster at Eton School, England

EXPERIENCE

You build it with blood sweat and tears, with joy and jubilation, with hard slog and/or freewheeling ease, all aspects that grow your skills and are visible are considered part of your experience. This is different from experiences which sometimes can have no lasting effect, they are just things that happen.

Experience is adding a new book in your library, a cherished object on the sideboard, an extra friend in your heart.
When you realise that you are gaining experience, then it will feel like you are finally doing the right thing.

Experience is me having had the ability to put on paper what I have lived up til now.

There are no useless experiences that teach you something, not even negative ones.
It is like a house: the foundations are first, then the bricks, one by one, set together with concrete. There is experience.

It is the baggage that we infuse in ourselves for what life and work have left us. Hyper positive experiences offer the euphoria of the moment. In moments of panic your heart goes into your throat and your legs give way, this point of view depends on your ability to see the glass half full or half empty.

There is a large suitcase, they deliver it to you when you are born, it's up to you to fill it and carry the burning heaviness or leave it empty and run towards nowhere.

Experience can be a hard teacher: you learn the lesson by walking through it.

EYE

It's a proven concept, you eat with your eyes first.
Eyes love the simplicity of beauty.
The sense of sight must be satisfied

But this meaning is not the only one.
We say: "it takes an eye" meaning to pay attention to details that cannot be left out.

Taking an eye in the dining room is mandatory, there are no shortcuts.
You can't pretend it's not important.
It can be a gift, a natural talent but it can also be learned, better, it must be learned, practiced and perfected over time.

It requires fierce effort to achieve the optimum level of attention to detail, but to hide the desired aim is like when dirt and dust are swept under the rug.

Develop your eye in a critical and constructive way, know how to be the careful teacher of yourself, direct your essence to attention and to discipline.
After practice you will find a glance is enough to discern what needs to be done..

FUTURE

Latin classics, mottos, sentences, idioms, proverbs, and fortune cookies. From the beginning of time we have known that the future is uncertain. The future is what is unknown. We can choose to fear it or look at with immense respect either way it can give us infinite emotions.
It's true, we'll never know what we will be able to achieve.
Yet there is a secret: letting go of the past and living in the present to finally welcome a bright future.
In the career of a waiter, one often wonders what will the future bring, whatever comes one thing is for sure, all our futures are different.

Any minute now we know we could be elsewhere or remain exactly where we are, maybe a new colleague is joining the brigade, or a customer we've never seen before is about to sit down at our table.
All this represents an unknown factor, but if we look forward confidently to the road ahead, then everything will be lighter.

It is not necessary to live believing that everything will be better, "the grass is always greener over there", it is infinitely more satisfying to live the present events and fully enjoy them.
"Life is What Happens To You While You're Busy Making Other Plans." — John Lennon.

When in front of us, on our plate, there is an amazing risotto, which intoxicates our taste buds, are we thinking of the next course?
Maybe so.

If so we are not giving the proper attention to this incredible risotto. Now what if the next dish is not good, we have wasted our opportunity to fully appreciate the risotto, the enjoyment lessened due to our lack of focus.
"Life moves pretty fast, if you don't stop and look around once in a while you might miss it" - Ferris Bueller
or more succinctly
Carpe Diem - Seize the Day!

GESTURE

The gesture can be understood in a physical or immaterial sense.

There is a basic body language that belongs to all of us and distinguishes us from others, each one of us has his own gestural expressiveness, sometimes imperceptible, subtle and light; sometimes bombastic with wild exaggerations. Often somewhere in between.
Even with these unique expressions there is common body language almost us all that can lead you to understanding the mood of a table without having to ask.

Bowed heads with arms crossed for example is not a good sign. Inversely a smile ,with hands held open, aimed towards the same table will usually bring heads up in anticipation, a good start to resolving any issue.

A gesture made with care towards the customer is like receiving an unexpected pastry, a sweet surprise. Gestures are important both to capture attention and to remain in someone's memory.

In Italy there are a multitude of hand gestures as an integral part of communication: there is no word or expression that cannot be accompanied by a gesture and it is what distinguishes us in the eyes of the world. India has a similarly co-dependant vocabulary with head movements, bobs and tilts adding extra meaning.

Often a gesture is worth a thousand words and creates a thin silk thread that embraces the diners, weaving the perfect canvas for the artist.

GOOD

Whenever I think of this adjective, the slogan used for so many Italian advertisements comes to mind: "mamma che buono!"   "mom, that's good!"

Because good is something that, inevitably, goes hand in hand with the simplicity of beauty, to fully enjoy something that makes us feel safe.
Good is therefore what we appreciate with the senses, yet the heart also plays its part.
Therefore good is also beautiful.

Goodness is an ancient concept and always appreciated. It is the most direct compliment a customer can give you. Although it is common and easy to say, it can make you feel great. You know that what he has been served has been better than just satisfactory.

Buono in Italian, Good in English, Bien in French, Хорошо in Russian, よし in Japanese, Güt in German... I was lucky enough to receive the compliment from customers of all nationalities, every time it was different every time it made me in tern feel good.

Because every good day is never the same day, every declination of the good is also different. It is repeatedly tasting the flavour of life and to affirm that, yes, everything deserves to be lived.

In a broader sense, as Pope Francis reminds us - *"Do not be afraid of goodness or even tenderness"*.

GRATIFICATION

According to Wikipedia, "gratification is the pleasant emotional reaction of happiness in response to the fulfilment of a desire or goal. It is also identified as a response deriving from the observance of social needs such as affiliation, socialisation, social approval and mutual recognition ".

I find the definitions useful, they manage to render in writing a feeling so intense that it seems ineffable.
Yet, can such a profound impression really be described?
Sure, you must have experienced it, perhaps every day if we can agree that the gratification, if we like the work we are doing, is a constant. It should also be read in the eyes of the customer who, in turn, will be gratified if we have been able to first meet our own standards.

Gratification is being pleased with what happens and it will be even greater if you let go of expectations and choose to enjoy the present, breathing deeply.

The secret for full satisfaction, both from the customer's and the team's point of view, lies in welcoming what happens. Don't be nervous or scared, this usually leads to mistakes. Be composed and confident in word and action, this sense of ownership will stop you from overreaching and keep the focus on what you can achieve easily.
This also brings with it the open mindedness needed to acquire new skills or improve the ones we have. It will be the way to better experience the events and joyfully perceive what surrounds us while welcoming the gratification of improving every day.

Showing gratitude to those in front of us or next to us is the way to abandon grudges.
We won't have grateful clients or colleagues if we don't show them the beauty of gratitude.
And for those who just don't want to know?
Let's get closer, do them a courtesy, then ask them for one in return: let's ask for a smile, he won't be able to say no.

GUEST

He is our ally.
It is a person who enjoys our hospitality.
Hospitality is offered and enjoyed.

This friend of ours has many faces he is a person who is invited to visit or stay in someone's home, also a person who is invited to a place or an event as a special honour.
But mostly for our purposes he or she is a customer at a hotel, restaurant or bar.
They are our guest.

Benjamin Franklin said - *"Guests, like fish, begin to smell after three days"* to indicate that a long stay ends up verging on harassment.
It makes me smile to remember it, however I have a different point of view.

Hosting is an art, being a guest is a golden opportunity.

"If you are invited to a dinner party you have a moral obligation to be amusing" - The Duchess of Windsor

It is the pure sense of conviviality, love given as a scented cloud.

It is our duty to envelop our guests in a secure cocoon of care and loving attention so as to bring the most amount of pleasure to their necessary act of eating dinner.

"Nothing would be more tiresome than eating and drinking if God had not made them pleasure as well as necessity" - Voltaire

HAPPINESS

What does happiness sound like?
There are so many nuances that it is perhaps impossible to give it a single definition.
To be honest I would like to rely on the discourse about happiness recorded on Italian TV by Roberto Benigni on Christmas Eve 2014,

In front of a moved audience, both in the studio and glued to their screen, he said-

"We always love too little and too late"

True.

But his passage on happiness is remarkable.

"Look for it, every day, continuously.
Whoever listens to me now is looking for happiness.
Now, in this very moment, because it's there.
Do you have it. We have it. Because they gave it to all of us.
They gave it to us as a gift when we were little.
They gave it to us as a gift, as a dowry.
And it was such a beautiful gift that we hid it like dogs do bone.

And many of us do it so well that we don't remember where they put it.
But we have it, you have it.
Look in all the closets, the shelves, the compartments of your soul.
Throw it all away.
The drawers, the bedside tables you have inside.
You will see that it comes out.
There is happiness.

And even if she forgets us, we must never forget her.
We must never be afraid of dying but should be terrified to never really live."

Happiness in our daily working life means not to be afraid to look in all those closets, shelves, behind the curtains or under the tablecloths, to reach the goal we have set ourselves: doing the job that, for us, is the most beautiful one in the world.

To allow us to really live and be happy.

HARMONY

There is nothing more satisfying for the eyes and spirit of a customer than seeing a dining room team working and moving in harmony. And not just in the eyes of the guests. For the Restaurant Manager too, he will see in that harmony the fruits of his effort, all the time and attention devoted to his duty of care.

Harmony during a service is made up of complicit glances between team members, they do not require words to understand each other, it's in the gestures of the hands that accompany each dish, it's in the restaurant spaces occupied at the right times and in the right ways, neither too much nor too little.

If I think of harmony, the image of the beehive comes to mind. It is the beauty of order. Every worker-bee knows exactly what to do and where to go. Each has his task and simply fulfils it without thinking that the work is exclusive, he does not know it, he is not aware of it. Yet harmony is inherent in his actions and in the place where he works.

Harmony is the deepest essence of this work. If chaos reigned in the room, the service would not be completed.

Harmony is pure poetry.

I'll leave you the three golden rules to make a perfect job, according to Albert Einstein -

"1. Out of clutter, find simplicity.
2. From discord, find harmony.
3. In the middle of difficulty lies the opportunity ".

HOTELLERIE

When I was little there was that game we called
"Names, things, cities ...".

It was a question of creating a group of friends, each had its own grid
and, having extracted a letter, each one had to insert in the grid the word
of that category that began with that letter.
Obviously some letters were more hostile. You had certainties: when you
extracted the "h", under things you could write 'hotel'.
Well, today I would write *'hotellerie'*.

So what is hotellerie, can we consider it a concrete thing?

Maybe, it's definitely a tangible concept. Maybe we can look at it as a con-
tainer.
It is also hospitality.

The hospitality, in our job includes all experiences from greeting to fa-
rewell and every part in between. We have the unique ability to cater to a
person's desires in a very bespoke way. It does not refer only to the extra-
luxury segment, you can also find it while camping. Any experience has an
amount of intangibles that can 'make or break' the clients enjoyment.

I believe hotellerie means "what you're looking for in a place to stay, that
feeling that you are home".

Elegant or comfortable, extravagant or essential: all can perfectly meet the
expectations of our guests if handled correctly.

Hotellerie is home. Home away from home.

INTERACTION

In physics, interaction means *"the transfer of energy between elementary particles or between an elementary particle and a field or between fields"*

More or less the same happens between people.

In the words of the sociologist Zygmunt Bauman -
"Spontaneous boundaries, consisting of the rejection of a commixture, unlike cement and barbed wire, have a double function: in addition to their purpose of separating, they also create defined boundaries between each other, thus having the role of being interfaces, promoting meetings, interactions and exchanges, and ultimately a fusion of cognitive horizons and everyday practices by their close proximity."

Just like that, in any restaurant service there is a "commixture" or a perennial meeting of totally different cultures, moods, smiles and tempers. We interact with each other is such a way that our ideas rub off on each other naturally, we learn good and bad habits just by our proximity to each other.

Our job is to exhibit the best behaviour we can for ourselves, we never know what others will adopt from our actions.

IRONY

Irony of being, irony of fate, fatal irony, vulgar and rude irony.
Good-natured, witty, bitter, cruel.
Reserve it, keep it with care, your irony.

For situations where there is a gap between reality and expectations, especially when a "hole" is created (to put it in journalistic terms) for another effect, I say let's use it.

The idea of irony comes from afar.
In Greek, eironéia means "dissimulation". It is the concealment of inventions.

But what is Irony.

Irony is when something happens that is the opposite of what was expected. It is one of the most misunderstood figures of speech in common English—many people think that the definition of irony has to do with coincidence or bad luck, when in fact it's more closely related to the subversion of expectations. There are three types of irony in the literary genre:

Verbal irony- is when a character says something that is different from what they really mean or how they really feel. If the intent of the irony is to mock or criticise, it is known as sarcasm. Be very aware of the difference between irony and sarcasm.

Situational irony- occurs when there is a difference between what is expected to happen and what actually happens. For example, a fire station burning down is a case of situational irony. Situational irony is the most difficult to influence but at the same time because it is decided by fate it is the most poignant. A situation in which something which was intended to have a particular result has the opposite or a very different result:

- *He noted with irony that the weapons were now being used against the country that*

produced them.

- It is one of the ironies of life that by the time you have earned enough money for the things you always wanted, you no longer have the energy to enjoy them.

Dramatic irony- Dramatic irony is when the audience knows more than the characters. The characters' actions have a different meaning for them than they do for the audience, which creates tension and suspense.

Sometimes we simply deal with something in an evasive way, going further, especially when work becomes heavy, better to add a pinch of irony, just enough, as we would find in a recipe.

Self-irony is an indispensable ingredient even when the situations that arise in a service can be unpleasant.
Learning to use it will be a fundamental element in our work.

JOURNEY

A journey starts with a single step, it arises from a remote desire or a spring strong enough to push us out of the familiar into the unknown.
A journey is also a trip inside ourselves, exactly as if it were the light of the union that brings with it a fire for the others as well.

Our journey is not only earthly, it is a sensorial experience.
There have been experienced travellers who got lost and some others who after a spontaneous trip, found themselves.

"Travel changes you. As you move through this life and this world you change things slightly, you leave marks behind, however small. And in return, life — and travel — leaves marks on you." - Anthony Bourdain

Every time I think about the value I give to travel, a myriad of experiences come to mind, heard told by past and present guests. Especially I think to my own travels.

I remember my first shift in a restaurant.
It is amazing how the first teachings, which we could consider initial, tiny, wavering steps, can be lessons for a thousand other experiences.
It would be a lie not to state that, at the first pat on the back that I was given, I felt, viscerally and infinitely elated.

During your journey you can receive recognition, esteem, yet the effort and the importance of leaving are not forgotten because they are the basis for a path.

Finally then the journey is the perception of what we like: a good wine, a slice of wholemeal bread, a well-seasoned agnolotto, the fragrance of a biscuit that reminds us of our grandmother or a familiar foreign courtesy, which somehow seems to be reminiscent of home …

JUDGEMENT

One day, while watching a talk show on television, the well known presenter said a useless sentence. I wasn't actually following the speech,I was watching the screen absently, lost in my thoughts, yet I was hit. She was arguing with another colleague trying to convince her that, although she was usually quick to make judgments other people, if necessary she would be perfectly capable of controlling herself and suspending judgment.
I wondered if I was able to suspend it.

We actually like it, it makes us feel better, to say that we do not judge, 'we're not that shallow', we condemn those who jump to conclusions or are quick to stereotype because the accusations usually have a negative connotation.
But it's an easy trap to fall into and on some level even if we don't say it, we think it.

The reality is this: the director of a team and a room, from the smallest and most modest to the largest and most opulent, must know how to suspend judgment.

We are certainly not talking about his objective assessment, since a comment given in full knowledge of the facts is often beneficial to everybody no matter how insensitive it seems.
We are instead discussing about the inability to control oneself and the tendency to judge situations negatively.
In a professional situation it shows lack of focus.

A good director judges positively what is good, objects to what doesn't work and finds the way and the words to deal with attitudes that are not appropriate.

A good director will know how to suspend the negative judgment, and with that he will know how to address any situation with flawless elegance.

KINDNESS

It is what must never be missing, particularly during a service at restaurant.

This book would not be possible without first conceding that kindness and love are key ingredients in every scenario on every page.

A loving, cordial, kind attitude is vital in the pursuit of the optimal, fine service.

We cannot be content to treating the kindness between guest and waiter, not even between waiter and waiter, not even between guest and guest. Kindness must be experienced first of all with ourselves.

In the Italian dictionary, at the word *"gentilezza"* (kindness), the second point is remarkable. It reads more or less like this
"the quality of being generous, helpful, and caring about other people, or an act showing this quality: kindness of appearance, kindness of manners; and in a moral sense: kindness of soul, of morals, of feelings. Most commonly amiability, politeness, courtesy in dealing with others".

In short, kindness ranges from grace to courtesy, to ways of expressing yourself, to your very behaviour.

Summing up: kindness is a super power.
Sometimes, some difficult situations, in which the customer is not particularly convinced, or a guy from the brigade has a disagreement with another, the use of kindness allows you to smooth out anger, to measure words, especially to use the right ones, words that will portray respect and courtesy.

Remember: Computers have no feelings, people do!

LANGUAGE

In short, a dissertation would not be enough for this term.

Language is one of man's most important inventions.
People use it to express themselves, to communicate, to deal, to love, to hate, to teach; to be individual.

You think: you draw up your thought: you speak.
There is nothing easier.
Flip the switches in your brain, evaluate if it is appropriate to speak, think about how to use the words then say them.
There's nothing harder.

Knowing how to use the most appropriate language in any situation is not a game.
Also language is not only verbal, it can also be non-verbal.
The language of gestures, of emotions, is visible to everyone, even to those who are blind from birth, because it is the language of feelings.

You may recall the literary passage from *"The Little Prince"* by Antoine de Saint - Exupery
"The most beautiful things in the world cannot be seen or touched, they are felt with the heart [...]the essential is invisible to the eye"

LEADERSHIP

It is a noun.

And then a stance, a pre-eminence, a guiding function towards a formation that, in other words, is a brigade of co-workers.

Yet a leader is always needed, even if perhaps it is better to call him director, someone who directs the group, who knows what is the best choice in that moment without being bossy, but authoritative. A conductor of the orchestra is the ultimate leader because without the players he is nothing, so too the restaurant manager.

This authority is not a sin, it's a talent.
All businesses or companies must have someone able to coordinate, to explain what is the best thing to do.

A leader is the person who best knows how to persuade other people to follow him, because he inspires trust and pushes action.
He is leading the race and in any case, he needs someone to listen to him.
Yet there is a price to pay, there is always something better to offer.
Many of the great leaders of the world have had moments of crisis, in which they thought that everything could subside; it was their followers who made it clear them that nothing would have fallen into oblivion.

And hence the real meaning: leadership is a "modus operandi", the state of mind of the whole brigade, it is knowing that only being together will we be able to get to the top of the podium.

The most beautiful music is made when the orchestra are in sync with the conductor.

LIGHTNESS

It cannot be bought.
It is sometimes difficult to find.
It is a state of mind.
I associate lightness with the pleasantness of dance, perhaps with butter-
flies. What is it lighter than a butterfly flying flower to flower?
This job can be stressful, obviously not often, but sometimes it can.

An impeccable service, be welcoming, be able to relate to someone's di-
sputes, yours and others' weakness: everything has the propensity to be
stressful.

Yet, lo and behold, we could choose to appear as light butterflies.
We could choose to be light ...

Lightness is inherent in each of us and must be sought, yearned for and
discovered.
It harkens back to being like children...

Being a source of concern for ourselves and for others can only lead us
to bad service.

So why don't we open that drawer and find lightness?
It is there, we have it, they gave it to us when we were little, then we bu-
ried it, for fear of losing it.

That feeling of lightness is not synonymous with foolishness, rather with
measured happiness. Keeping a lightness of spirit means you can shrug
off the small annoyances of others while also recovering from your own
small stumbles quickly and with a graceful demeanour.

Muhammad Ali was saying more about this lightness of spirit than his
boxing prowess where he said - *"Float like a butterfly, sting like a bee, his
hands can't hit what his eyes can't see."*

To be light means making peace with your heart, dancing among the tables, since also air is fully breathable.

The customer doesn't care for your troubles, the customer asks for attention, friendliness and lightness.
Look deeply into his eyes ... Let the sadness go and make the most of every day!

LISTENING

Listening is different from hearing. You can hear a myriad of gossip, you can hear the voices of people, the horns of cars, the chirping of birds, the idle chatter of strangers in waiting rooms.

Every day the the world round us makes it more and more difficult to really listen: we are surrounded by couples who during a dinner prefer to scroll through the posts of unknown people on Instagram rather than talking to each other.

Noise and frenzy flatten the world: it is deafening, it cannot be heard. Sometimes we are so focused on the goal that we forget to listen to what's actually going on. The most important thing, in this as in all jobs, is to communicate and listen, especially to what is not expressed in words. A customer's gaze, a colleague's pout, you need to listen to everything.

An example: How many times in the past week have you actively listened to customers, colleagues, bosses or collaborators? Be honest. If you are still thinking about it, it means that you have not done it enough. I repeat: hearing is not the same as listening.

Actively listening tom someone is giving them your undivided attention, sensitivity and intelligence. We are equipped with it, use it. You'll be surprised at how much easier it is to fulfil someones desires if you truly listen to their request.

LOVE

It takes love to do this job. It takes love to fully dedicate yourself to guests.

Many times we read that passion is necessary for this profession. It's not true. Passion is not enough.
It's like a love affair.
Passion is the initial feeling, burning desire which keeps us awake until morning. To make the story last there must be love.
It is love that makes us understand and accept the small weaknesses of others.

And so it is for this profession: you will often think that the hours spent working are a lot, that many times your patience is brought to the limit, that you have not been able to spend a family holiday or that you have not been able to see a concert on Saturday night. But sooner or later these hardened feelings of lost opportunity will fade. This is the moment when the passion for our work passes and leaves room for love.

Love your job and every moment of it: from mise en place to last goodbye, from moments of joy to those of discouragement. Only in this way can you give love to your guests.

Serving is, in itself, an act of love.

MANUAL SKILLS

Manual dexterity brings our mind back to something physical, something real.
Fortunately, nowadays, our society is returning to its origins, to the use of hands. The master craftsman, the artisan, the value of ancient or not so ancient techniques too important to let slip away, if only because skilled work is a valuable commodity. Appreciate the craftsmen and women who make the most premium whisky or wine, caviar or fine hand-made chocolates.

For a long time, having manual skills didn't lead to big luck.
My life experiences, to whom it may concern, have always admired manual skills: knowing how to do, create and shape exactly like a demiurge does in his forge.
The demiurge is a philosophical and at the same time mythological figure, he is a divine being, endowed with a creative and generating capacity, described for the first time by Plato in the Timaeus.

I have always been very fascinated by artisans, those who actually create something tangible.

One day, thinking about this book, I felt disjointed: I had writing everywhere, some post-its with definitions even came up from drawers; honestly, I still didn't quite know what they were for.
Then it happened I met a blacksmith, a craftsman. I don't know why but he told me that he often created random pieces, without knowing what to do with them; later they had come in handy and he had found a place for everything.

It was then that I realised that, in my work, I too felt a bit like the demiurge of myself, of my condition, of what I did every day: in any case, thanks to the commitment and some effort , everything would fall into place, everything would take a shape, it would be moulded perfectly to what I meant.
So it

MATURITY

You'll reach it, certainly everyone, sooner or later, gets there.

When is your time? No one knows.

What then in short.
Are there so many differences between a man and an apple?
Maybe: the apple is juicier.

Joking aside, the human being, like everything in nature, needs time, nourishment, rain and sun to mature and reach the fullness of his form.

If each of us undertakes to live the natural rhythm without tending to "take shortcuts", surely we will have a more aware and fuller maturity.

Returning to nature:
I like spring because the days get long and the sun warms more intensely. You can see the peach orchards in bloom with a pale pink, at times more intense, preceding juicy, ripe and sweet peaches.
What would happen if we harvest a peach that is not yet ready? We would risk breaking our teeth and ruining our mouths for the sour taste.

Here. Maturity is waiting for the right moment.

Maturity is knowing how to grasp the important side of life, the sweetness of being, and at what time.

MEMORY

There are those who boast a mind like a steel trap and those who can't remember their own phone number.

Have you ever dwelled on the many advertisements on television that promise a better memory?
That's because it is extremely important and we would all like to recall facts instantly. But it is not always possible, it is not always feasible.
Experiences, sensations, real life stories are stored in ours brain and constitute a historical memory.
Sometimes the mind processes and distorts memories - there can be a certain charm behind all this.

But lets leave the charming embellishment of our memories alone for now and let's instead focus on how important it is that we remember customers.
In the era of smart phones no-one can be criticised for not recalling phone numbers anymore, technology, such as directories or files, can help our memory. That is a good thing.

Why is it so important to remember?
Because each of us needs to feel important, because we want to be sure that the other is considering us, he remember our personal tastes, which table is our favourite in the restaurant, he didn't forget the wine we appreciated so much on our last visit.
Memory is closely related to taste because we ourselves tend not to pay attention to the names, specifically of dishes or drinks; what we know is that we liked them very much, that they fully satisfied our taste.

And what do we expect from a good waiter?
May he remember them for us, so that he can welcome us every day, offering us the certainty of feeling pampered.

I have overheard many people refer to their favourite restaurant as the one where *"they call me by name"*, I'm sure you have too.

MISTAKES

Small and easily repairable or huge and catastrophic, there is no getting around the fact that mistakes will be made.

Sometimes we even don't notice making them, other times its not our fault, still others it is but there's nothing we can do about it.

Mistakes remind me of my teacher's red pen, when inevitably the red strokes maddeningly invaded my work.
Who hasn't this happened to?
Yet, thanks to the school, I have this memory.

Error comes from the Latin error. Derivation of errare or *"wander, roam, ramble"*.
Originally, therefore, it meant a diversion, but also a journey, a stroll with no fixed destination.

The most bizarre notions are always those we remember the clearest.
After all, the mistake is also a journey, even in a workplace, some of the best ideas come from mistakes.

In 1972, Mirko Stocchetto at the Bar Basso in Milan added sparkling wine instead of gin to a Negroni. He realised that this variation had some sense and his humble mistake led to the creation of a classic cocktail that is still enjoyed all around the world today, and to its name: in fact, in Italian "sbagliato" means mistaken.

When you're wrong, you try to learn from your mistakes, sometimes you do it again, but not often twice and almost never three times. Learning this way is sometimes the best and often the only way.

Obviously, managing your own or others' mistakes is never easy and it takes the right tact to point out when a co-worker has done something wrong, at the same time it is necessary to make him understand how he can improve, what is the right way to learn something, and not repeat it.

"Don't lie about it. You made a mistake. Admit it and move on." - Anthony Bourdain

An error can also be made by the customer, certainly in good faith. Even then, you can't be rash. Basically, I believe that error is human, just manage it with confidence and humility.
The customer isn't always right but they don't necessarily need to be made aware of this fact.

Gianni Rodari said: *"Mistakes are necessary, as useful as bread, and often beautiful: just look at the Tower of Pisa."*

MOMENT

"And later on, when so many roads open up before you, you don't know which to take, don't pick one at random; sit down and wait. Breathe deeply, trustingly, the way you breathed on the day when you came into the world, don't let anything distract you, wait and wait some more. Stay still, be quiet, and listen to your heart. Then, when it speaks, get up and go where it leads you."

These are the very last lines that precede the abandonment, the end of the novel "Follow Your Heart" by Susanna Tamaro. There is the right time for everything, and there is no need to exceed in haste.

The future is ours.
The future is uncertain, as the past has gone, now battered by time.
The moment is that moment in which the lungs inflate and deflate, the breath becomes intense and we welcome what is around us.

And so let's start from the first meaning.
The right time is always what we are experiencing. Also, it's the time we have to confidently wait for, hoping right things will happen, without treading too hard.
In the dining room, the right moment is what you perceive on your skin, you know at that moment you will have to act in that given way because experience has matured in you the exact response to the moment.

I think the very famous Carpe Diem, too often translated as "seize the day", has a much more intense meaning. It is a cry to grab every moment, of every day, with every bone in your body.

There is no escape, in our work we need to be ready. It is knowing at any moment it will be the right time. It is one of the first pillars to inculcate in a new staff member.
I often reiterate that everything lies in paying sensitivity even to a minute, because the moment is not measurable, the moment is what you live by listening to that inner voice that tells you: *"it's time, go, now is your time ..."*.

122

MOTIVATION

There is always a motivation, it is the engine that drives the world.
One of the engines, however it is relevant.
Without a real motivation, sometimes, you don't move.

The French writer Antoine de Saint-Exupery stated - *"If you want to build a ship, don't waste your time calling people to gather wood and prepare tools; don't distribute tasks, don't organise work. Awaken in them a yearning for the distant and boundless sea, when this thirst has fully taken hold they will immediately set to boat-building."*

Before you even start doing a job, you need to be motivated to do it.
We cannot argue about which spark has ignited the right motivation, everyone has their own. The drive towards perfection is a solo journey, but one that can be shared in spirit with your team as the results are part of the same goal, even if the motivation to get there is different for all.

Motivation is inspiration, it is enthusiasm, it is something that is associated with a constructive action. Your motivation needs to come at least partly from the customer, who has chosen your restaurant to enjoy his time.
This motivation must drive each member of the brigade, since this will guide towards forming all tasks with an eye to an all-round service.

Being motivated is staying focused on what you are doing, without being distracted by anything else.

An unmotivated person watches a gust of wind, the motivated one does not feel even the storm, he is too busy flying kites.

MULTITASKING

In Italian it is "multi-process" which, from information technology, indicates the ability of a software to run multiple programs simultaneously.

Man is made of flesh and blood, yet he may be able to "perform" multiple activities at the same time. We can say that the "multitasking" of the human being is a capacity.

The modern world travels very fast.
Work, life, free time: everything is concentrated in too short a time.
In the service it is mandatory to develop the ability to do several things at the same time, especially to see and know how to read different situations.

Whoever manages to be efficiently multitasking during work, is not a superhero: they simply use concentration well to stay focused on the targeted goal; the bigger picture is made up of many parts and it's easier to keep these parts moving in the right direction when you see the way they fit together as a whole.

Concentration must be a mantra, a simple thing to repeat and repeat again.

The moment we focus on the goal knowing it is our primary aim, then we will know how to turn all our will towards it and we will achieve achieve that goal.

This does not mean to praise the hectic life, simply a spur to abandon distractions at work, ignore the chatter that clouds the mind and be "on the spot" with heart, mind and emotions. With focus.

NO

No. No. No.

No, is a word that you can never use to a customer.

There is always a way.

Saying no at first glance means immediate closure: it is a decision that will make us appear unprepared.

An immediate negative will drive a wedge between us and the customer, better to say yes then work out how to make yes happen, even if the solution is very different from the guests request it is better to offer another positive solution than a 'no'.

Our simple fear is enough to lose confidence and esteem in his eyes, no means "i can't do it" in a room where you should be in total control.

I am a manager, a waiter, a friend and a confidant.

I'm at the helm of a brigade and fleets of patrons that stand in front of me every day.

I have a duty to give certainties and opportunities. And it's actually a pleasure to do so.

There is no place in life for uncertainty: give emotions!

NOVELTY

It is the lifeblood that allows you to savour the beauty of the world.

This is what entices the customer, even the most regular guest is looking for something new in the experience, a new dish, different wine by glass, new staff, anything to keep the experience dynamic.

New. Just the word alone is intriguing.

The novelty enchants you, surprises you.

When something new is proposed it is always a pleasure: for those who do it and for those who receive it.

Novelty is a word that works by itself.
Novelty conquers minds and hearts.
Novelty is hope, it is new, it is the expanding of horizons.
Novelty is the road less travelled, it is innovation.

The customer in your room will not be able to resist.

Constant evolution is no less important for us either, to keep the crew engaged, excited.

Innovation is something beautiful.
It is a new concept, made from scratch, different from the usual.
The novelty is, in itself, interesting.
Novelty is pure originality.

OPINIONS

Wikipedia says: *"The term opinion (from the Latin opinio, -onis; in Greek dòxa) generically expresses a judgment, viewpoint, or statement that is not conclusive as apposed to facts which are true statements"*

Opinion leads us, often in good faith, to judge a personal or collective version of a fact to be true and, while not excluding the possibility of being deceived, the same fact is evaluated as authentic until proven otherwise.
I would add that the opinion is mine, yours, ours and theirs.
Opinion is like taste, everyone's s different.
That almost all of our insecurities stem from our concern over other people's opinion is certainly true.

Yet, if we all had clear-cut and truthful opinions there would be no more discussion. The harsh truth, while often seen as inconsiderate, verging on mean, is undeniably what the person believes to be true and this arrests all speculation by its sheer bluntness. Why lie if you're just going to piss someone off anyway, right?

We must avoid being rude but our opinion must be expressed with acuity and intelligence. When a viewpoint is formulated and spoken casually or without sincerity it is futile.
Knowing how to give a right opinion in the right way is knowing how to stay in the world walking on your own legs.

ORGANISATION

It's all about planning and careful execution.
Without structure our very existence would be unthinkable, there would only be chaos.

Organisation is that feeling when you know you are prepared at your best, you planned everything; if accidents happen, you will be ready, or at least you will have created the conditions to do your best.
Organisation is not just something scientific, it is rather practical: it is conceiving an idea through the human spirit.

If it were just a matter of structures and procedures, then any unexpected issue, particularly during a frenzied service, should make our professional facade start to crack.
If we used in our daily work all the lessons, all the routines, all the skills we have learnt so far, then organisation will come by itself, it will become the way of operating that is naturally part of our being.

In every organised situation there is always someone who knows perfectly what is his task: it is the role of a leader to know everyones part and make sure they are prepared and able to carry it out, he cannot afford to make mistakes or lose attention because with him the entire team triumphs or fails.

Being organised does not mean causing the destruction of ourselves and others by micro-management and unreasonable workloads, rather it is to be standing in the right place at the right time. Of being thoroughly prepared.

PASSION

Love is the core of what we do, passion feeds it.

It seems incredible to say yet passion is sometimes physical suffering, a deep and tormenting affliction, a beauty that is released in a moment or for a specific reason in our life.

Passion can also be an inclination: in this case the passion for service, cooking, wine, etiquette and hospitality.
With passion, the intensity of feeling spreads into our daily life.

Passion is an attitude.
Passion is generated out of love or out of anger.

Nothing would exist in the world if there was no passion.

It is she who allows us to get up in the morning with the tremendous desire to do the thinks we love.

Without it everything would seem empty.
Passion makes us forget we're tired, it keeps us from being complacent or bored at work.
To live, it takes passion.

The first breath we took, as soon as we came into the world, was a breath of passion.

PATIENCE

Holy patience.

When you think you have run out, you discover, 'Hallelujah' there is a fraction left, that it has not vanished: the reserves are there and they are tangible.
We are safe, our patience has been been tested, and it has triumphed!

Joking aside, for those who work constantly in contact with the public, patience is a necessity. A gift we are provided with.

When you are in the dining room it is an invitation to moderation, to a pleasant endurance, to a tolerance of your fellow man that is intrinsically linked to courtesy.

Patience is not unique. Patience is offered and required.

We all wish there were never any hitches or delays in service but there are.

Starting from the assumption that none of us in the morning is called to get up and save the world (at least not in this profession) we need to learn to use our super powers and with a certain presence to ourselves, use them in the best way.
When regular or even occasional waiting is a certainty, waiting patiently is a virtue

There is no profession that doesn't need some patience, surely there are those that require infinite.

If you too work in a restaurant, if you have had the patience to read up to this point, it means you have plenty.

PEOPLE

I always like to start from the idea that we are all equal, each with their own joys, their pains, their more or less heavy everyday life, a home, a family, a car, passions and affections.

We are people, human beings: all with different strengths and weaknesses but with the same curiosity for life.

I like this job because I can meet and get to know people who are very different from each other, especially in terms of their origin: each one tells his story, his truth, critical or not, we embrace each other, sometimes we clash: but that is all extremely human.

People are to be loved, they are not objects, they cannot be exploited or taken advantage of, and this is especially true in the workplace.

It is a question of "you scratch my back, I'll scratch yours", the important thing is that no one forgets that the other is also made of flesh and blood, has his own emotions and his weaknesses. The easiest rule to follow is the old adage- *'treat someone the way you want to be treated.'*

A company works when you can trust those around you and there is the possibility of leaning on the other, especially in difficulties.

I believe in people with keen eyes, tuned ears, work-soaked hands, clear minds, a strong beating heart, fast legs and slow tongues.

I believe in those who have their own personality. But not in those who have more than one.

I believe in those who have the ability to love, meet and savour discovery without fear and without barriers, as if they always tend to the island of their dreams.

POSITIVITY

Bombarded with miracle cures, pills, potions, diets, exercise routines, meditation and so on; all promising health and happiness; at school or at work we often pretend to be incurably negative, a way to squeeze sympathy from everyday routine.

Because the antagonist of positivity, negativity, has become a lifestyle. Why focus on being positive when society, in all reality, asks us for widespread negativism? We compulsively search, especially through search engines, how to find that elusive happiness.

When and why did we lose sight of positivity and its faithful companion, happiness? When we were little we just waited for the afternoon homework to finish to go and play, we focused on the happiness in the very moment we started doing what we wanted.

That's really all it is: being active satisfies us, make us positive and happy. Positivity, optimism and satisfaction are closely related.

"Make time for yourself. Exercise does not deplete my energy. Instead, it gives me energy and makes me feel like a young kid again. Throughout my travels, I make time for physical activity, preferably a fun group exercise. Having fun with others makes exercise feel less like a burden and more social." - Sir Richard Branson

We work in an active social environment and can take Sir Richard's advice into the workplace easily.

Be positive and get up in the morning thinking that we will soon start doing what we are meant to do, join the workplace with a smile, welcome the customer looking him in the eye, keep the red thread of happiness always well tense, so that it does not run the risk of tearing itself apart, falling back into the abyss of darkness.

PRACTICALITY

Practicality, thirty years ago I structured mine.
That practical sense that came to my rescue so much throughout my life, today translates into the practical 3.0 sense, the mental one.

Practicality is a gift.
Yet, after spending a lot of time using it to get out of trouble, you need to learn how to apply it.

I remember someone once said there is a practical aspect to my designs, and I remember thinking, 'That doesn't sound very creative,' but that is actually the truth. There is a practicality to it. I don't design just to design. There is a reason and, hopefully, an interesting reason behind it - that is where my creativity comes in. - Kate Spade

You must remember how much it served you.
You must remember that it is there, it stays there and observes you: it never leaves you.

Practicality is adaptation, being able to find the most suitable answers in every circumstance.

Sometimes the customer demands speed in elucidating a certain dilemma's outcome and, only by mediating with practicality, can the answer be fulfilled.
There are very fast seconds, in which time is not enough.
There are eternally long seconds that seem to drag on indefinately, in which we would just like to run away from the embarrassment of the moment.

We are not always ready, that's true. Unfortunately, in our job, this is not allowed.
We need to be on point, no ifs or buts.

Learn physical practicality, then learn to use it through other faculties.
Practicality safeguards against crisis.

PREPARATION

Extremely useful, especially in schools.
But not only that, the preparation is useful in all cultural and professional areas.

In 1907, Baden-Powell, an English soldier, devised the Boy Scout motto:
"Be Prepared". He published it in Scouting for Boys in 1908, in the hand-
book he defined the motto that to Be Prepared means *"you are always in a
state of readiness in mind and body to do your duty."*

In fact, yes, you have to be ready in every moment of life.

You have to be ready to handle even an unexpected situation, from missing place at table to a dish that doesn't satisfy your guest, beware and
prepared not to lose your temper and to portray a readiness to solve any
problem that arrises with competence that comes from thorough preparation. .

Prepared and curious, always on the move because basic knowledge is
not enough, you need a constant dose of desire to learn, learn, grow,
renew yourself, believe ...

PRESENCE

Presence is something that is owed, above all, to oneself.
Being present to yourself means living the here and now without frills, or unnecessary trappings. The presence is a courtly cuddle that is due, first of all, to us. The moment you are present with yourself then you will also be present for others. In the dining room it is essential to be there: to be present for the customer, for your team and for the environment itself.
Even in personal relationships, we know how much non-presence costs, which is in no uncertain terms, absence.

Absence is something that creates a void. Absence is not being there. Absence is not being present. This means that we do not attend to the expectations of those in front of us.

Colleagues and especially the customer need us, just as we all need everyone. There are no excuses You need to be present with your mind and heart, and be there in the best possible way.

How many times have we heard it said: *"That man has a beautiful presence"*?
Well, I don't think it's just an aesthetic question, but when we talk about good looks it's because we're referring to a beautiful person maybe outside, especially inside.

Sir Thomas Overbury in his poem *"A Wife"* (1613) wrote *"All the carnal beauty of my wife is but skin-deep"* Meaning, external attractiveness has no relation to goodness or essential quality.
His prose has been often rephrased as - *"beauty is only skin deep, real character is to the bone"*

The smile, the posture, the look and also the thoughts that we emanate ensure that our presence is pleasing to others as well as ourselves.

While I was finalising what I might write about presence, I came across a phrase from Lao Tzu, a Chinese philosopher, which sounds more or less like this:

"When he is born, man is soft and weak; in death he becomes stiff and hard. The ten thousand creatures and all plants and trees while they are alive are supple and soft, but when and dead they become brittle and dry. Truly, what is stiff and hard is a "companion of death"; what is soft and weak is a "companion of life". Therefore "the weapon that is too hard will be broken, the tree that has the hardest wood will be cut down". Truly, the hard and mighty are cast down; the soft and weak set on high".

What to do with it?

I believe that beautiful presence is also this: a bath of humility.

Being soft, if defined as being pure of spirit, then yes, it can be a good way to be an excellent presence.

PROBLEM SOLVING

What does problem solving mean?
It is finding the solution to a problem, possibly finding the best solution.
In polished terms: it is an expression that indicates the necessary technique to the analysis of a problematic situation to implement a solution.

The question: is it a natural talent or can it be learned?
I think they can both be true. Let's say, if it's a natural talent, the way will definitely be downhill.

Restaurant service is made up of fleeting moments.
Let's start from here.
When a job is made up of moments, the error margin must be narrow, almost non-existent.

In the presence of a table full of hungry customers, full of expectations, a problem is the archenemy, yet it can happen, there can be issues that arise.

How to solve them?
It is easy, you simply don't make your customer aware, in any way.

"Dirty washing should be laundered at home"

So the brigade problems or hitches will be handled internally, without those at the table perceiving it.

Our ability to solve problems quickly and quietly is a sign of a professional team and should be worn as a badge of honour.

PROFESSION

It must be taken seriously.
We are professionals.

Here the Earth is not saved, it's used, and this must be done in the best possible way.
There is no way to take your profession lightly, whatever it is.

From the blacksmith to the carpenter, lawyer to clerk, the teacher to the waiter, it is necessary to safeguard what one is and what one does.
Producing work for ourselves and for others in the generation of home delivery pizza and internet shopping seems an antiquated mentality, the problem is laziness but also fear.

We must work on our way of doing things in order to fight those who call our profession into question.
Sometime you may ask yourself-
Why do I approach this job reluctantly?
Why don't I put my all into this profession?

Sometimes it may be that this is not the job for you; sometime you've just had a bad day.
So why continue on this road, there are countless others …?

I serve because this is my life, my choice came first (but perhaps actually it is hospitality that has chosen me, fortunately!).

Restaurant service is hard, it is necessary to have a particular conception of events that must be carried out in the appropriate way, otherwise it is just a revolving door of strangers that we don't really care about and, I think, having this in front of you every day is not really living.

You must embrace this profession with your whole heart in order to reach the top, if you cannot you must admit your limitations for advancement and be happy with this or change career.

PSYCHOLOGY

It is the greatest intangible gift of a modern waiter.

Being able to interpret the state of mind of the person next to us, or the customer in front of us, is essential for understanding their needs and emotions.
Perceiving their mood, can help you empathise.

Psychology is made up of sounds and looks.

To feel is experiencing the other, living in his dimension.
Without interference.
Welcome it as if you are welcoming yourself.

Look at his eyes, his hands, his gestures.
Everything communicates something. Stay there, observe, as if it were forever.

Drawing his psychological profile is highly respectful, it means that you wish to take care of him.

The service must fit the customer like a tailored suit: neither one centimetre less nor one more. This is why I like to define us as gastronomic tailors.
The Maitre' is always a guide, for the brigade as well as for the diner.

QUALITY

Quality goes hand in hand with excellence.
A guarantee is basically a quality certificate.

Here the aspects of a reality that is subject to judgment are assessed.
Good, bad, poor, valuable or commendable.

Quality is then still a leap, therefore a change for the better of something or situation, of a person.
Quality is a classification that is sometimes opposed to quantity.
That famous saying - *"I prefer quality over quantity"*.

And it is fundamentally so, especially in this work.

Quality is a gift.
Quality is intrinsic and extrinsic to the product.
In other words: the quality is in the product and exactly one step further.

Quality is understanding what the other is looking for in order to fulfil in the best way.

"Be the yardstick of quality. Some people are not used to an environment where excellence is constantly expected" - Steve Jobs

RELAXATION

I believe that the word relaxation has been abused.

We are surrounded by people who wait for the weekend to relax a bit and then frantically going to do the autumn, spring and pre-Christmas cleaning, or spend their time off shopping wild and senseless. Who go out to nightclubs to dance, drink and party as a way of unwinding but this isn't relaxation; I as far as the body and mind are concerned it is sport.

Relaxation is a serious matter, it has a very specific meaning that is not to be wasted. Having some relaxation is important for the mind and body,
it is not a joke.
Perhaps there is a lot of talk about it because it has recently the concept of 'a relaxed state of mind' and meditation through phone apps is trendy.

So why run endlessly without relaxing?
We are trapped in a society that considers relaxation a dirty word, that says if you have time to relax you're not working hard enough *"gotta make that money!"*
This is actually very dangerous.

Relax, recollect, take all other thoughts away from you. This is true relaxation: letting the world around us fade into infinity. But how do we switch off?

There are no rules.

Well....maybe just one.
Learning to be with ourselves in peace and tranquility, that's what relaxation is for me.

Wellness centres, restaurants, the places where we operate are trying to instil a sense of pure and true relaxation. This is often not considered by the client himself, because he is unable to relax.

If a client of mine were in front of me right now, I would say he can rest assured, I will serve him as best I can, I will offer him all the love in the world and infuse him with all the light I have.

I offer him a moment of relaxation.
It is the highest gift I can offer.

RESPECT

It must be given and demanded.

It is obvious that a waiter has to offer its maximum respect to the clients, who must on their part offer it back where deserved; the same has to happen among co-workers.
If each of us started from the assumption that the life of every living being is sacred and precious, that we must "respect" it, then we would stop dividing the world into classes, by age groups or gender, between religions, between those who respect and those who don't. If everyone is respectful of others these distinctions disappear.

Respect must be known and used.

There are no two ways, half terms or otherwise about it; this is the basis of a loving society: without it we can only speak of rough relationships.

Treat others with dignity and appreciate the diversity of those in front of us, and this then increases respect for ourselves.

"I don't have to agree with you to like you or respect you." -Anthony Bourdain.

We may not agree with what we are told, with the criticism that has been levelled, however we must defend the opinion of others in every way.

Sometimes I believe that we should respect our neighbour even a little more than ourselves. Because we cannot choose who we will meet to-morrow, we know who we are facing today, for this we can only say that we are grateful and ensure a respectful approach to everyone.

RESPONSIBILITY

It costs. It weighs on us. We earn it. It rewards us..
It seems like an oxymoron doesn't it?

Responsibility is built, created, sweated over, bled on, fought for and even accidentally acquired but it all feels the same. It is yours to protect as only you can destroy it.
It is not given to you, you simply feel it, you perceive it, above all you build it within yourself, step by step, mistake after mistake.
It is necessary to be congruent with the commitment that one assumes.

Once the path to be taken has been chosen, it must be pursued, and yes, it is your responsibility to make this so. There is no improvisation, in life there is one and only one way: preparation.

To be prepared, it is not enough to just study although this is the first step in our journey, you also need to understand the strength of what you have to do. This comes with experience, usually with failure and the lessons that come from that failure.
In the dining room, being responsible for your station means just that, being prepared and not leaving the facts to chance.

It is not possible, it is impossible, we must always know what we are doing, where we want to lead the customer and our brigade.

It's all summed up in being responsible professionals and, even more so, responsible men and women of the restaurant floor.

It also implies the acceptance of every consequence, since one assumes once one takes on the responsibility of a task one takes charge of the situation.

Responsibility is worn like a wetsuit, a second skin.
Responsibility is a path that presupposes rules.

REVIEW

Never before have reviews been so popular or easily accessible than right now.
The term has its roots in ancient times, from the word 'recensere', "to examine", this term was used to describe the publisher's job of editing his writers words before they were published. To criticise and correct before the work was presented to the public.

Times have changed.

Now a review is most often a critical examination in the form of a comment on social media not actually an article in book, magazine or newspaper and can be of anything: a film, a dinner plate, an ice cream cone, a bus ride, a view of the mountains, the list is endless: there is no object, place, restaurant, monument or person that cannot be reviewed.

In a world where social networks rule, where do-it-yourself reviews are everywhere, it is essential to understand when and how they can be considered reliable.
Reliability reigns supreme; only by verifying that the source of the review is objective and trustworthy can we actually understand if what we are reading is true.

The actress Claudia Cardinale, referring to the writer Pier Paolo Pasolini, in 1938 stated: *"I met him when he was a screenwriter: I saw him often, for example, at the time when I was playing Il bell'Antonio. [...] I owe him my first, authoritative, positive review [for the role in Un maledetto imbroglio]: he wrote beautiful things about me, and, as usual, absolutely not trivial. I consider that review my first, true, consecration as an actress".*

I often hold performance reviews of my staff for the purpose of guiding them towards improvement by an honest account of their daily work, much like a director does with his actors.

RHYTHM

It takes rhythm. The right pace.

Never be too accelerated or sluggish.

The pace to be adopted is your best step forward within your group.

Wikipedia has this definition: *"Rhythm is a succession of sound events with inherent durations and possible pauses, spaced in the time domain from a few tenths of a second to a few seconds, which usually but not necessarily follow one or more cyclical patterns . It is also used to distinguish one note from another "*

Every musician, singer or dancer must have a keen sense of rhythm.

Rhythm, for a waiter, is the energy that flows in the veins.
It is the passion of a dream that is crowned in the work, to observe a brigade moving in sync is like being at a rock concert, tapping your foot to the beat.

It's selecting the right gear while we're driving, using common sense. If used well, it becomes second nature.

It's having the rhythm in your blood to not even think about it anymore.

A salsa dancer knows the steps by heart and acts, dances to the music, knows she is doing the right thing.

Personally I'm not a very good dancer, but I know the rhythm of the restaurant by heart.

RIGOUR

We come to rigour.

Bear with me here; I thought of football.
Of the penalty kick which, according to Wikipedia, is *"the restart of the game used when a player commits an offence against an opponent, in his own penalty area and with the ball in play, he is awarded a direct free kick."*.

Well, although bizarre, the example is fitting.
In sport or in any other activity, there are regulations, which require compliance with rigour.
Rigour is knowing the rules of the game and applying them.

If we want to be rigorous, it means applying a certain rigidity towards ourselves, a hardness or even harshness if you will.

This leads to a lot of discipline, precision and consistency, above all with this work, since in a dining room being scrupulous, abandoning the neglect and imprecision is essential.
Imagine a restaurant where the rules are abolished, where everything is allowed: things cannot work.

Each staff member must be rigorous for himself and for others.
Where there is no rigour, there is no good service.
If everyone is not his own master, he cannot serve others respectfully.

RULES

Hard. Often raw.
Always definitive.
Rules must be respected if you want to play the game, in fact without them there is no game.

Even in the dining room, service is performed by a team: each has a specific role, must keep his place, must not abandon his teammates.
He knows that whatever happens, he will have to try to do his best. In case he falls short, he can count on the rest of the staff, on the manager and on the customer's "clemency". Without rules you cannot reach your goals, you cannot be even a little lenient, especially with yourself.
Anarchy creates disorder.

I often and willingly ask myself what are the precise rules to follow: certainly for the mise en place, the clothing, courtesy and modus operandi must follow the classicism of the old school.
For the rest, a margin of personal expression remains.

I use a metaphor - The most harmonious materials are the malleable ones. The inflexible ones are so stubborn that they break if stressed too much.

In a delicate job like ours, where one shift is different from the other as is each customer, to be resistant, staying firm on one's own convictions does not exactly mean to go by the book.
Understanding when it is time "to soften rules" is essential, so we can avoid of messing up a service and breaking the link among collaborators or customers.
The rules of the service? Study them, know them, apply them, modify them, update them.
About service rules, François Pipala, historical maitre at L'Auberge du Pont de Collonges by Bocuse family, says-
"It is not about serving from the right or from the left, the matter is to always serve from the proper side".

SATISFACTION

It is pleasure.
It is a sense of contentment.

"Open your eyes, look within. Are you satisfied with the life you're livin'?" Sang Bob Marley.

Satisfaction draws its nourishment from many areas that we can deduce: one is the professional one ... And it is a question that each of us asks himself almost every day: am I satisfied?
The fact is that we are not happy even when we have done our work flawlessly, rather we want immediately the next service is even better.

What's wrong with this step?
Who has the authority to push us to satisfaction?
Only we can do it, no one else.

The secret lies in gratitude, not because it makes success easier, but in analysing what we have accomplished we discover the secret of our satisfaction; the nuances of it.

Satisfaction is to be found in guest's eyes who takes his leave pleased.
Satisfaction is in tired feet late at night.
Satisfaction is in the thoughts that accompany the working day.

We must be stoic and control ourselves, governing our satisfaction consciously.
The question to ask ourselves is: did I give my all?
If the answer is yes, then we can be satisfied.
It is not possible to guide colleagues and guests if, first of all, we do not govern ourselves.

The art of contentment is the recognition that the most satisfying and most dependably refreshing experiences in life lie not in the great things but in little ones.

SERVICE

It is the key noun.

Already from the title, even before the writing started, service was the focal point.

Mine is not just a job, because serving is a modus vivendi - literally *'a way of living'*

I like to do it daily, calmly, without pompous ceremony and avoiding arrogance when something is actually going very well.

Whatever goal you reach in life, know that you will have to stay connected to your roots, with the people who taught you the trade. Stay grounded even when your dreams are in the heavens, because there will always be something even more beautiful to aspire to.

My tail swells like a peacock, however, when I tell about it, all this, and I say with pride that serving, being at the service of guests, does not mean being servile.

Service is everything for a man in the dining room. It is life blood. It is light.
To serve is to put our whole existence to impart a soulful experience to all those who cross our doorstep and welcome them as friends.

SITUATION

For this exercise let's think about an awkward situation.

The term "situation" can sometimes, but definitely not always, be used to describe something negative that is happening.

We do not know why, it is the moment we are in, it is here and now.

I remember a sermon from Pope Francis in which he said that we have to focus our attention to the present because the past has been and gone, the future is uncertain and then the only important thing is what we are experiencing, our situation right now.

Matthew the Evangelist then recalls that *"every day has its own cure"*, this means that we should not worry too much about tomorrow, because while we may have many troubles today, there is a solution to any bad situation if we focus on what's in front of us and don't stress the unknown.

A situation is the circumstances we find ourselves in..

Any situation should be handled as any event that happens, it is not necessarily negative, it may also be positive. Even the bad ones can be improved if looked at from the right perspective.

Each situation evolves according to our experience and the ability to move forward.

We know perfectly well that if we don't take care of her, she will go against us, if instead we lovingly understand her as something manageable, then she will be able to give us a solution more easily.

There will come a day when, thanks to experience, you will not only be able to make a situation evolve, but you will be able to create it.

And there it will be fun. That's where the beauty of this work begins.

SMILES

They costs little, are almost always free to give…why then do we often avoid spreading them, they're somehow a little scary or embarrassing.

An acquaintance of mine says that you should always smile, even when you don't want to, even when you don't want to smile at yourself, you should stand in front of a mirror and smile at yourself.

I do that!
Unfortunately to often this society has a default scowl rather than smile and it scares me, but honestly, and to quote the iconic phrase uttered by Rhett Butler, played by actor Clark Gable, in the film Gone with the Wind, in 1939 - *"Frankly my dear, I don't give a damn!"*

You see…

We must not abandon our smile for without it our friends will not have our silent support in troubled times, a small gesture for sure but a smile at the right time can lift someone instantly and without words. A smile in the dining room is a secret weapon, quietly overcoming tension and doubt; secretly letting others know you are on their side.

A smile, in our work, is a beautiful business card.
A business card that can make us memorable.
A fond memory that doesn't take much.

Never forget to smile.

SPEED

The world we live in is fast.

The speed I mean is not the stressful one in the world, it is the practical speed of problem solving, the ability, not to be unprepared, to instead have good improvisation skills.
To work fast and hard without making mistakes.

Being fast and clean in the room is not easy.

Going around the problem, dribbling useless intentions, won't make us impeccable waiters, rather crude confused impostors.

Boring the customer with long, useless, verbose stories will divert attention from the real protagonist of the meal, the customer himself.

Speed demands organisation.

To be fast means to perceive the right pace, understand when it's time to speed up or slow down, it is knowing how to capture in a flash a need and infuse it with all the energies we have.

Sometimes the mind will travel at the speed of light, some others the legs will have to eat up the road.
Human speed is not technological acceleration, rather it is the ability to operate the mind and body at the same time.

My old mentor used to say *"less speed more haste"*, a confusing adage at the best of times.
What he meant was "If you go too quickly you will make mistakes and a mess, the same task at the correct pace will cut down on errors and clean up; actually taking you less time to complete in the end."

STORY

Stories are reminiscent of our grandparents, sometimes even mum or dad, but parents are often too busy with other matters to have time to tell them as much as we wanted as kids.

The story refers to the memory because it is something that is imprinted in the mind and we never forget it. It can be passed through generations and become fable, or just be personal to you. A good story has the ability to teach and entertain; above all this is what we look for because they are the ones we remember.

I believe that everyone has their own memory capacity: there are those who say that when they read something they do not forget it, others that if they see an image they will remember it for life, still others that when they hear someone speak they will retain what's said easily.

I was telling my experiences to a journalist, I noticed that she wasn't writing my thoughts and, at first glance, I was almost annoyed, I thought she didn't care. At a certain point I had to ask, politely of course, if she would remember everything, she told me that she remembered all the interviews she had done, she would never forget until her mind, perhaps due to old age, would give way.

It impressed me a lot and I noticed a certain similarity with my own memory but in my case I remember everything that customers order or the passions they have, for the simple fear of forgetting, in reality I never forget, I know perfectly well the essence of their story.

Because the story, whether true or fictional, is a slice of life, it is something that will always remain with us if it is well told. To remember facts we must put them into context with our situation; we must tell ourselves a compelling story so as to not forget the pertinent facts.

STRENGTH

It is enough to truly consider the word "strength" to immediately feel its effect, either weakening or giving power to your condition. The power of a word.
Power can be uncontrollable, wild and indomitable. Sometimes low, flat, depressing.

Like with weight training a small increase of effort daily seems less arduous than tackling a huge weight straight away, the same can be said for mental strength. Although physical strengthen can be an advantage in the restaurant industry we will keep this discussion to mental fortitude which is essential.
What is important is what you put into it. Positive thinking is a powerful tool.

"What does not kill me makes me stronger"- Friedrich Nietzsche.

This concept can be applied in the dining room: we are constantly exposed to great pressures and yet you cannot give in, you continue to serve doing the best of your ability. Basically this work is made up of initiation rites that can lead to brave, tenacious people with a solid character and plenty of scars.

"Skills can be taught. Character you either have or you don't have." - Anthony Bourdain

"Just because you are a character doesn't mean you have character" - Mr Wolf, Pulp Fiction

And then the strength of our hearts will make a big difference: for this reason it will guarantee us a stronger sensitivity.
Sensitivity and strength go hand in hand, they must be used in equal measure.

Over the years I believe I have developed an inner strength that allows me to have the right energy every day, but I don't forget the initial difficulties, of all the times the room put me to the test.

Trust me it gets easier.

STRESS

It is the opposite of a nice Sunday drive in the country, of an evening spent in a cozy room by a crackling fire, while perhaps outside the window you can see the snow gently falling. It is enemy number one of a good book, of a full-bodied glass of wine half drunk, of the pleasantness of loved ones company, of contemplating a sunrise or sunset, of walking barefoot on the beach, skipping stones.

Stress is the greatest evil of this society.

You can be more or less anxious, more or less stressed. But it doesn't depend on us, because the world around us almost seems to revel in whipping along on at it's frantic pace.
The images we see every day are of frustrated people who splash from one metro station to another, of road rage in a 2 minute traffic jam who then get angry at not finding parking space assuming they'll be late for work, people gripped by the fear of even returning home because it is not possible to relax there either.

Stress is less than useless, it is outright damaging.

It may seem trivial, yet it is a golden rule to be applied to both professional and family life. We will not be happy with our parents, siblings, wife, or husband if all we do is start a stressful fire when we return home.

We will not be good waiters serving stress.
In the room there can be no room for this negativism, because it challenges the harmony we strive for so intently. We must let our traveling companions taste how beautiful this work is, and let our customers enjoy how much they deserve to be with us.
There are so many stressful things in our guests lives already we must not pile more on, we must take their anxiety away for a few minutes or hours in the hope that when they leave they enter the world calmer. Relaxed. At least for a little while.

SURPRISE

Everybody likes it.

It is a breath of fresh air through the room, blowing dust off the furnishings and cobwebs from the mind.

There is surprise is in a plate, in a bottle of wine, in a song from the past.

It is a surprise is to bring the customer his favourite dessert, without him knowing it, to welcome him with good news.

Surprise is that instant emotion that makes us rejoice, opens the heart. Surprises make us feel loved and considered; the customer must be surprised continuously, surprised and not shocked.

There is something ancestral in all this, it harkens back to childhood. Whoever is not able to be surprised means that they have grown too much, so much that they have 'seen it all before', one hopes this is actually kind of true and it's not just a loss of the sense of adventure that make surprises fun.

Children no, they know how to remain in open-mouthed bewilderment, always.
Maybe the secret is to grow up remembering what it means to be a kid. Childlike not childish.

"The greatest joy is that which was not expected" Sophocles said.

I love getting up in the morning, opening the windows and looking outside.
When the weather is dull I am disappointed, I don't appreciate it.
But if the morning is sunny, I breathe and I open my mouth wide, I know how to become a kid again.

SYMPATHY

A sympathetic person is one who's motivated by compassion, one who can empathise with another and support them. Usually sympathy is offered to others who are suffering, and while of course this is the correct way to behave, we can adopt this outlook towards any situation in the dining room.

Feeling sympathy for someone is extremely positive because it's a surface-level acknowledgment of someone's feelings or a situation that they're going through. Good or bad.
Being sympathetic is about saying, *"I hear you, and I value what you're feeling."*

Hateful are those who are not sympathetic by nature but who try to be so for fun or profit..

A sympathetic eye is not learned but it is a card to play with the customer, if you have it.
Be careful, however, to know how heavy to apply it to each situation. It can appear fake if applied too liberally.

A common mistake is playing the classic funny guys with the customer , this is terribly bad taste and you risk running into unpleasant situations. Annoying the customer, so to speak, is just around the corner.

Furthermore, it is necessary to measure sympathy in general, more than anything to feel sympathy for ourselves, to ask ourselves are we content, then ask ourselves what could make us happier and nicer

Thanks to sympathy we can better communicate with people and with our own soul, because it is a good and genuine ingredient which, if added in the right quantity, adds flavour to any dish.

TALENT

If you have it, and you know it, then you need to find somewhere to apply it.

Being talented is knowing how to draw the clouds of the sky, the sun, perceive the scents of nature, make a dress, write a poem, describe a wine, prepare a good sandwich for your children, play the guitar, know how to hug people, paint a landscape, talk in public, serve well at the table also being a good cook.

Being talented is composing music, snipping haircuts, carving wood, forming iron, clay, or glass, knowing how to make concrete, being a good politician (an almost un reachable talent), so come to think of it is volunteering but it shouldn't be,. Some have a talent for being alone, taking an exam at the university, writing an exam for students at the university, making an espresso, telling a story.

Being talented is making use of the positive sides that exist in us.
Self-dilapidation is often ferocious.
Don't worry, it is not true that your passions (not skills) are zero, each one does not have a thousand, he has his own. Your skills may be different from your passion, in fact it is often the things we can't do that we most admire.

Each of us has their particular dreams placed randomly in the drawer, each with its own rhythm.
Each of us has their own talent.

TASTE

Each his own. Not all flavours are mint ...
It is extremely subjective, there is infinite space for imagination.

Your taste is an identity card, it could be included in your curriculum vitae, sometimes it is so unconscious that you don't even know it fully. Everyone has different tastes, food and especially wine can taste different to different people because flavour is to a large extent memory. We associate memories to flavours and smells more than any other sense and of course the experience must change depending on each persons experiences.

It is too easy to be led into an opinion by others who appear more knowledgeable, I urge you all to discover your own tastes, your own flavour palette, to truly explore the flavour combinations that are pleasurable to you - life will be much more enjoyable if you do.

"Some people have such good taste they can't enjoy anything." - Marty Rubin

Wikipedia offers us this result: "Taste is one of the senses, whose receptors are the taste buds present in the taste buds of the tongue, soft palate, pharynx, cheeks and epiglottis. Taste depends on the synergistic perception of five basic tastes: bitter, sour, sweet, salty and umami; some research suggests the existence of a sixth and seventh fundamental taste associated with fried and fat ".
And therefore taste depends on the synergistic perception of five senses.

I say that taste also depends on the heart.
There is a particular phrase by Marcel Proust contained in 'À la recherche du temps perdu' that recalls a journey. In the text we find a crucial phase:

"The only real journey, the only bath of youth, would be not to go to new landscapes, but to have other eyes, to see the universe with the eyes of another, of a hundred others, to see the hundred universes that each one sees, that everyone is ".

Travel?
Yes, because taste is a journey.
A journey into one's existence, into present, past and future life.

"Travel isn't always pretty. It isn't always comfortable. Sometimes it hurts, it even breaks your heart. But that's okay. The journey changes you; it should change you. It leaves marks on your memory, on your consciousness, on your heart, and on your body. You take something with you. Hopefully, you leave something good behind." - Anthony Bourdain

TEACHING

To teach: from Old English tæcan *'show, present, point out'*, of Germanic origin.

The same is in Italian language: the term insegnare comes from the Latin docere 'to show, to indicate'.

In this work one thrives on instruction, it's a constant perpetuation of knowledge, skills and ideas.

I remember my first job as a waiter, already mentioned in another definition: my maitre endeavoured to teach me the best way to do this job, sometimes he did it directly, sometimes indirectly.

Certainly it was not easy. For him, I mean.

There are good teachers and bad teachers; good students and not so good. That's a lot of variables attached to your learning ability, I was somewhere in the middle, not great not horrible but the effort I put in, the dedication to my craft helped raise the experience. Some of my lessons were coming from people who weren't interested in teaching me. Through laziness, time restraints or they just weren't good at it.

Very often I puzzle out about what is the best way to educate budding young people who want to become good waiters.

Where's the truth?
I don't even know, I only have my experience, the load of know-how that I myself have learned and common sense.

'You can teach a person all you know, but only experience will convince him that what you say is true.' – Richelle E. Goodrich

Teaching is giving you the means to prove for yourself what has only been hearsay until that point.

190

TEAM

It is a group of people who work together to achieve goals.
Each has their strengths, weaknesses, obsessions, skills and passions.
Everyone puts their emotions on the line, without sparing themselves.

Sometimes I imagine myself on the set of the film *'Any Given Sunday'*.
Directed by Oliver Stone and played by a masterful Al Pacino.

What person, at least once in their life, would not have wanted to be the coach who incites the team to victory with a speech that goes down in history?

"I don't know what to say, really. Three minutes to the biggest battle of our professional lives. All comes down to today, and either, we heal as a team, or we're gonna crumble. Inch by inch, play by play. Until we're finished. We're in hell right now, gentlemen. Believe me. And, we can stay here, get the shit kicked out of us, or we can fight our way back into the light. We can climb outta hell... one inch at a time.

Now I can't do it for you, I'm too old. I look around, I see these young faces and I think, I've made every wrong choice a middle-aged man can make. I've pissed away all my money, believe it or not. I chased off anyone who's ever loved me. And lately, I can't even stand the face I see in the mirror.

You know, when you get old, in life, things get taken from you. I mean that's a part of life. But, you only learn that when you start losin' stuff. You find out life's this game of inches, so is football. Because in either game – life or football – the margin for error is so small. I mean, one half a step too late or too early and you don't quite make it. One half second too slow, too fast and you don't quite catch it. The inches we need are everywhere around us. They're in every break of the game, every minute, every second.

On this team we fight for that inch. On this team we tear ourselves and everyone else around us to pieces for that inch. We claw with our fingernails for that inch. Because we know when we add up all those inches that's gonna make the f***king difference between WINNING and LOSING, between LIVING and DYING!

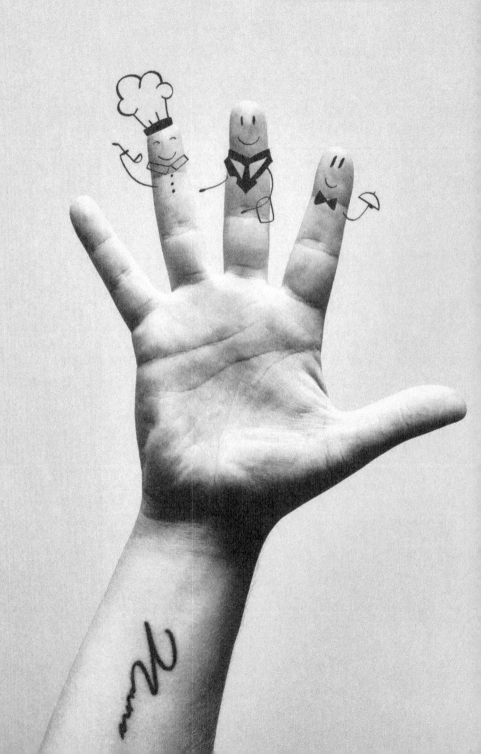

I'll tell you this, in any fight it's the guy whose willing to die whose gonna win that inch. And I know, if I'm gonna have any life anymore it's because I'm still willing to fight and die for that inch, because that's what living is, the six inches in front of your face. Now I can't make you do it. You've got to look at the guy next to you, look into his eyes. Now I think you're going to see a guy who will go that inch with you. Your gonna see a guy who will sacrifice himself for this team, because he knows when it comes down to it your gonna do the same for him.

That's a team, gentlemen, and either, we heal, now, as a team, or we will die as individuals. That's football guys, that's all it is. Now, what are you gonna do?"

It is not that I lacked the words to talk about team, I simply couldn't say it any better than Al Pacino and knowing your limitations is part of teamwork too.

TENACITY

Tenacity is gritting your teeth and getting it done!
Tenacity is a love story to your ambition.

Alda Merini, one of the truest poets ever seen, one day wrote a poem entitled 'I have known wonders in you', it sounded like this -

"I have known the wonders in you
wonders of love so discovered
that looked like shells to me
where I smelled the sea and the deserted
flowing beaches and love inside
I am lost as in the storm
always holding this heart still
who (well I knew) loved a chimera ".

When we persevere at work, infinite secrets can be discovered.
Every lunch, every dinner, any service requires a good dose of tenacity.
We need to push ourselves out of our comfort zone in order to discover where our limit is.
To reach our goals and surpass them takes tenacity.
As they say at the gym - *"no pain, no gain"*

The beginning, the apprenticeship, then the rise to always be something more and better , to manage the restaurant maybe oneway to own one yourself. All improvements are linked to being persistent, to not giving up, smelling and listening to what the customer is asking of us, going the extra mile, accomplishing the next step, the next goal.

Our guest does not know that we are resilient, that to offer him exactly what he needs, in life, we do not back down, we persevere.
We reach new heights not even we knew were possible.

He doesn't know how tiring it is: yet only in this way, only by giving that one hundred and one percent, will he have a colourful memory of us, of the dishes, of the wine, of the place, of our effort.

"If you feel safe in the area you're working in, you're not working in the right area. Always go a little further into the water than you feel you're capable of being in. Go a little bit out of your depth. And when you don't feel that your feet are quite touching the bottom, you're just about in the right place to do something exciting." - David Bowie

THOUGHT

Positive, captivating, meaningless, good, bad, risky, funny, sad.
I seriously think that this is the most difficult definition I need to put into words because thought has a thousand facets, there are many ways to use it and there are millions of ways of thinking
Everyone has their own thought.

René Descartes said *"I think therefore I am"* and it's hard to disprove his philosophy as our thoughts define us as people, everyone behaves differently, to a large extent, because they have unique thoughts.
You have yours.
I have mine.
But what is thought actually?

If I think about it, my elementary school teacher comes to mind when, instead of boring math homework, he set us creative writing tests.

"Write 10 thoughts. 10 sentences, for tomorrow," he said.

And so, the most absurd banalities started to form in my mind because, you know, when something is imposed on you, it is not really creative, it does not lead you to dream.
So I ended up writing about how beautiful my day at school was, what I did with my parents last Sunday, what I would like to receive from Santa (maybe a dog), and so on.

Then you grow up and realise how much thoughts affect your mind and your body.

I remember reading some time ago in a holistic book about the cause of ailments and how they are generated. I dwelled on the belly: it was said that gaining weight was a consequence of the fact that we held on to past grudges, that everything is concentrated in the fat.

Given that, doing this job, I know well that eating often leads to gaining weight (however eating is also one of pleasures in life, I mean come on!), yet I really liked the idea that thoughts could affect one's being.

This was an important turning point: I would train myself to think positively even in the most negative of situations.
My thoughts are, and they must be, always positive since I need to be a better man, every day.

TRAINING

It is fundamental and must be continuous.
You never stop learning, ever, even if you reach higher and higher peaks, yet there is still much to aim for. What a boring place perfection must be because there is no more discovery left.

Anyone who thinks that job training is frivolous or a waste of time can definitely stop working right now.
Without trying to scare you away, I must stress, training means instilling passion in what we do, being passionate, wanting to learn more and more to give our best.

These days the market offers continuing innovations, jobs evolve, customers' needs change, we ourselves change. Technology and the almost unlimited access to information is speeding up the innovation process, we must keep up or be left behind.
Being trained means keeping a watchful eye on what's going on around you.
It is knowing how to be in a context using what we value and not abusing what, actually, we don't know.
It is being relevant.
Stable on constantly shifting ground.
Being trained means being ready, prepared to face everyday situations so as not to sink into the boorish habit of always doing the same and identical things, it allows us to be dynamic.

You have to know the rules before you can break them.
But what does that mean?
My music teacher once asked the class:

"How many of you know your major scales?"
It was a simple question and nearly everyone raised their hands right away. Know them or not, no one wanted to look left behind.
"Alright, pretty good, but how many of you really know your scales?"

A few of us continued to timidly raise our hands. I quietly thought to myself, *"Well, I have all my scales memorised, I just have to think a little more on the hard ones, but I still know them."*
"No, no, how many of you know your scales?"
Instead of waiting for any of us to answer, he picked up his trumpet and ran through every major scale up and down the horn at lightning speed. Then he started playing them in 3rds and 4ths, and in triads and arpeggios.
Point taken. In most of our young minds a scale was 8 notes in order and "knowing" that scale meant playing it slowly with some mistakes. However, without any words exchanged, we witnessed what it truly meant to know your scales. From that moment on the definition of "knowing your scales" was forever changed in our minds – the bar was raised.

"Learn the rules like a pro so you can break them like an artist" - Pablo Picasso

TRATTORIA

It is the place of the heart.

It is the welcome on Sunday at mum or grandma's house, right before lunch.

A Trattoria in Italy is one of the most beautifully simple pleasures. It is a restaurant but it owes its heritage to a home kitchen. The menu is most likely to be made from Granny's recipes if not by the matriarch herself. It is charmingly homey, welcoming and cosy. It is comfort food that is extremely specific to the area.

The trattoria is the stalwart of our culinary tradition, the beacon to which all Italian cooking is aimed.

Italy is the homeland of hospitality and, by osmosis, of the trattoria.

Without trattorias we would not know where to find home-made tastes, nor would Italy be recognised as a food and wine ambassador of the world.

In a Trattoria you will find traditions like wine from the barrel, meat cooked over open coals, homemade pasta, salamis aged in the restaurant cellar, home baked bread and hand-made tarts with fresh jam from the family orchard. Trattorias proudly fly the flag of Italian gastronomy

The French, our cousins of the Alps, boast the grandeur of service, Italians have the cacophonous warmth of people eating and laughing around a table. Grand but in a more relaxed and familial way than the French. This is the allure of a trattoria.

And lets not forget that emblematic character of the restaurant, the host.

A good host knows your tastes, knows what your favourite dishes are, what your favourite table is. A good host knows your name. The host has an eye, ear and memory.

All waiters in Italy have a small part of the Trattoria host in them.
It is their charm.

TRICKS

I'm talking about the classic tricks, the oldest in the book, the tricks of the trade. Nobody will tell you which are his, it seems obvious that the first trick to perfect is to steal with the eyes. To observe others and learn their secrets.

There is no fixed rule, each brigade finds its own: a point in the room where you can have a better view, to hear more clearly what is happening, a location for the service station that has everything on hand.
A smell of frying garlic and onions, sizzling pan walked through the dining room, this was a trick my old chef used to sell more appetisers.
The tricks are subjective, they are the expression of ourselves.

Sometimes we need to be helped by memory, at other times by what technology offers us, like remembering what the customer likes by drawing up a spreadsheet, a digital file, a post-it note.
At this point, do you remember what I wrote above; up there in the second line?

"Nobody will tell you their tricks"

This is 90% true because your manager will induce you to discover his, you will have to capture them, observe his techniques. It's like a passing of knowledge.
If it were a story, this would be a snippet of Vincenzo's -

I remember that, very young, I started my service in the dining room.

I remember when, still very young, I started serving in the dining room.
The maitre began, obviously without telling me, to shake crumbs from the dirty tablecloths behind the curtains, where, if I hadn't been careful, I never would have found them; and I didn't.
It was just like that for a couple of times, then I understood, it didn't take long: he wanted to push me to observation.
His trick worked.

UNITY

There is an old adage about breaking sticks. You can snap them individually over your knee one by one but bunch them together and they will never break.
It is the famous one about strength in unity.

You know it, don't you?

The expression is a metaphor for a group that works closely together, while also focused on the goal.

Imagining a room that is about to prepare the room in a disintegrated form, therefore without union, one can see the potential for catastrophe. I believe that unity is the fulcrum: it must be set, precise, organised and true. Its centre is the director of the hall who will always be the glue between brigade members.

A smiling and exuberant team, who work well together as a well oiled machine will instil tranquility in the customer. This is a confirmed fact.

In a dining room, scents, colours and sounds flutter like a light echo and blend in a deep and clear union. They become one, complete. After all, this work is characterised by the union of satisfying moments too: just when you start and end together, following a path.

Walter Philip Reuther was an American leader of organised labor and civil rights in the mid 50s and he said - *"There is no power in the world that can stop the forward march of free men and women when they are joined in the solidarity of human brotherhood."*

He was a union man.

He also said - *"There is no greater calling than to serve your fellow men and there is no greater satisfaction than to have done it well."*

He would have made a fine restaurant man too!

VISION

A view of things, of customers and colleagues, a worldview.
Vision of the family, of one's private love and work lives.

Viewing is, first of all, the way we read what happens in our daily life.
Being a visionary means having an open, clear-headed and witty mind to
seize opportunities and choose the best path to take.

There is no dichotomy between the two statements: they must be a perfect combination that reinforces the meaning itself.

Vision is an art: that of seeing even what cannot be seen.
If we can see invisible things, then we will be able to reach the unattai-
nable.

Vision often goes hand in hand with the whimsical power of madness.
Visionaries are daydreamers who perceive the imperceptible.
Those who cannot be a visionary will never have the privilege of having
and giving their best in their work and letting it drive them ever so
slightly, ever so poetically, mad.

WAITER

By definition it is a worker who performs their tasks privately or in public places. True. Unassailable.
The reality is that the professional waiter today must be so much more.

What if I told you that the waiter would need notions of psychology, comedy, empathy, a sense of the tragic and basic notions of baby and dog sitting?
Are you smiling?
Well, that would be incorrect because yes, these would be needed, but it would take many, many more. He must be a good valet, know foreign languages, have a sense of order, discipline, good taste, humour, measure, savoir faire and beyond.

The waiter observes our tastes and traits, our birthdays and anniversaries, our wives and (ahem…) girlfriends birthdays and jealously guards them in secret diaries.
He knows how to be, when necessary, a silent judge of character and/or keeper of secrets.

No, it's not your wives or girlfriends who know you best:
It is your waiter.

WARMTH

It brings to mind the flames of the fireplace, a mother's kiss or the hug of a small and chubby child. Heat is physical.

But it's not just caresses. In the dining room it's how we make our customers feel, how much attention we offer them, what subtle methods we implement to make them feel better, feel at home, the decisions we make to ensure the right level of pampering.

Think of an after-dinner chocolate paired with coffee. Honestly, I'm not used to the chocolate-coffee combination because, in short, I don't love it, yet when they offer it to me I feel happily welcomed. A banality? I don't believe it is when a feeling of warmth is the result.

The value of a frank smile given to the customer is immeasurable. Sometimes it radiates more than the sun and moves more than the stars, it is a way to make our presence felt in a genuinely loving way. Human warmth shines, it makes us shine but it is not learned: it is possessed or not.

Our warmth towards another must be genuine to be believed. if forced it is dishonest and almost always this has the exact opposite effect as intended.

"*Love restores like the warmth of the sun after rain*" wrote William Shakespeare.

WILLPOWER

Almost nothing is impossible if you have force of will.

If what we do is our dream, what we are suited for, then it will not be difficult to find the will to continue.

Yet it may be that you loose that urge. Some may discover a new calling while others just gradually shift focus. This is natural and normal, we are human.

We are not the same as 20 years ago, in 20 years we will not be those of today.
There will have been peaks and troughs, stressful low periods and fervent, euphoric highs.

Our willpower is that essential component that allows you to climb the mountain, without ever losing sight of the peak

Then it is useless to bask in nothingness, to argue we will never be able to bring this or that it to completion. Will is a weapon, a state of mind in which we repeat *"I've got this!"*, it is hard, of course but the results are worth it.

This work is a game. Not a simple or a difficult game, but a game.

Do you remember when you were little and spent hours and hours, concentrating, to play? Was it hard work?
Not at all, it was a way to not notice the time passing, to have fun. In the end you were satisfied because you had spent the time doing something you liked, you had succeeded while having fun.

So?
So you applied willpower without even realising it.
To do your job well, become a child again, start playing.

WORDS

Words, words, words.
You need to know how to measure them.

Also, to be monitored is your presence at the table.
Perfect ingredients, words and presence, but they are to be mixed with care.
Any excess could be harmful and lead to a guest who does not enjoy our approach any more..

Also, never flaunt knowledge that you do not have with customers.

Words can be the key to breaking into the customer's heart and capturing his attention.

Using terms like "seasonality", "cooked by the chef for you", "our latest innovation from the kitchen" can bear good fruit.

When addressing a guest it is necessary to use the philosophy of 'less is more'. While this is a phrase that many have made their own, it was coined by the German architect Ludwig Mies van der Rohe and also calls for simplicity in the construction.

Being good speakers means saying the right concepts at the right time, ranting is counterproductive.

Speak to welcome the other, not to cause him to faint.

WORK

Hard, rewarding, excellent, well or poorly done, amazing, exciting, boring, more than hard, daily, non-stop, with or without a coffee break, accompanied by more or less enthusiastic colleagues, exhausting, mandatory.

We could add infinite adjectives to the noun work, either positive or negatives.
But the only one for us, perhaps, is daily.

Without cynicism, I quote the words by French writer Gustave Flaubert: *"After all the work is still the best way to pass life".*
And this is indeed the case, working is a means of spending seconds, minutes, hours, days, months and years in the best possible way.

What does it mean to do a fulfilling job?
It is having the determination to put your feet off the bed and walk lightly because, even today, we will be lead actors in the dining room.

Today is different from yesterday and tomorrow too will be different ...

A customer we haven't seen for a long time, an unexpected meeting that opens our hearts, our team's esteem, a guest's approval, even a criticism, an element to improve the service: everything contributes to ensuring that every moment is worth living.

At night, in the dark, each one in his bed hugging his pillow, we understand if the day just passed was spent well or badly: if the stomach and heart are calm, it means that we are doing what we are meant for. Doing it well.

In his book "Fai bei sogni", the journalist and writer Massimo Gramellini writes: *"If a dream is your dream, the one you came into the world for, you can spend your life hiding it behind a cloud of skepticism, you will never get rid of it.
It will continue to send you desperate signals, such as boredom and lack of enthusiasm, trusting in your rebellion".*

ZERO

I repeat: zero.

Zero is the number of mornings I woke up without wanting to go to work.

Zero is the number of mornings I woke up thinking I wasn't giving my best to myself and to the guests.

Zero is the number of mornings I woke up and thought being a waiter was beneath me.

Zero. Year zero. Number zero.

Like this book. Like a new birth.
Because the time had come to tell what being part of a restaurant staff means.
My job, your job, our work.

ACKNOWLEGMENTS

Many thanks to Sara Checchi, Tatiana Donatiello, Simonetta Nave, Francesca Gerbi, Carlo Spallanzani, Fulvio Zendrini and all those who supported me and made possible the realization of this book.

Printed in Great Britain
by Amazon